"Oh, a ten-dollar hoss and
A forty-dollar saddle,
And I'm going to punchin'
Texas cattle."
　　　　—*The Old Chisholm Trail*

illustrated by Dale Crawford

$10 Horse, $40 Saddle

Cowboy Clothing, Arms, Tools and Horse Gear of the 1880's

by

Don Rickey, Jr.

Introduction to the Bison Books Edition by
Daniel N. Vichorek

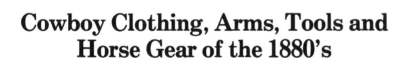

UNIVERSITY OF NEBRASKA PRESS • LINCOLN AND LONDON

First Bison Books printing: 1999
Most recent printing indicated by the last digit below:
10   9   8   7   6   5   4   3   2   1

Library of Congress Cataloging-in-Publication Data
Rickey, Don.
$10 horse, $40 saddle: cowboy clothing, arms, tools, and horse gear of the 1880's /
by Don Rickey, Jr.; introduction to the Bison Books ed. by Daniel N. Vichorek.
p.   cm.
Originally published: Ft. Collins, Colo.: Old Army Press, c1976.
Includes bibliographical references (p.   ).
ISBN 0-8032-8977-4 (pa.: alk. paper)
1. Americana—West (U.S.)   2. Cowboys—Costume—West (U.S.)   3. Firearms—
West (U.S.)   4. West (U.S.)—History—1860–1890.   I. Title.   II. Title: Ten dollar
horse, forty dollar saddle.
F594.R527   1999
978—dc21
99-18169   CIP

Reprinted from the original 1976 edition by the Old Army Press, Ft. Collins CO.
This Bison Books edition follows the original in beginning the introduction on
arabic page 8; no material has been omitted.

Introduction

Daniel N. Vichorek

Years ago when I was a sort of government-employed saddle bum, I noticed that a brass cinch ring on my government-issue saddle bore the inscription: "Pat'd, 1819."

That was in the 1960s when the world seemed to be coming apart. All the old American assumptions were in question and the very nature of reality seemed uncertain. I found it comforting at the time to think that at least there was some stability in the equipment used to fit the rear end of a human to the back of a horse. Don Rickey's book, *$10 Horse, $40 Saddle* sometimes surprises us by how much has changed, and sometimes by how much has remained the same since the 1880s.

Consider the yellow slicker, for example. Rickey notes that the oilskin slicker tied behind the saddle was essential to every 1880s cowboy. He notes that a few black slickers crept in, but these had drawbacks and were not favored. He also describes the slicker as being designed to cover the rider and saddle. The price in those days was $3.50, about ten percent of a cowboy's monthly salary.

To this day, if one were to gain a high point on a drizzly day when cattle were being moved far out on the plains, the eye would be drawn to the only vivid color in the landscape; bright yellow slickers covering riders and saddles. As in earlier times, other colors are available, but not favored. These days, instead of oilskin, slickers are vinyl, made in China, but they still serve the purpose. The price is up to $35, maybe five percent of a cowboy's wage.

Other accouterments began changing even before the 1880s were fulfilled. The cowboy saddle, for example. That torture device, seen today in about any history museum in the west, is so painful to contemplate that even the most ironbound traditionalist is not tempted to mount it. Experienced riders look at the tall horn rising like a slim desert butte from the narrow fork, and they wince. The cowboy saddle started evolving beyond that painful stage in the early nineties. Today's saddles with their swell-forks and wide seats look like easy chairs by comparison to the museum pieces. "Back in those days you had to know how to ride," as one survivor of the old era said.

The cowboy saddle of the plains normally was double-rigged— meaning it had two cinches, one fore and one aft, which gave a better anchor when roping an ornery critter and seizing the rope around the horn. These double-rigged outfits were referred to as "rimfire," after the double firing pin that was used in the rimfire rifles of the time. Single-cinched rigs were used west of the Divide in Oregon and Idaho, and some of these migrated to the plains. They were said to be "centerfire." Rickey shows how these two types evolved into the "Montana type."

The rimfire saddle was one of the items that came north with the herds from Texas in the big drives that started in 1876 (except for Nelson Story, who did it in 1866). The Texas cowboys brought with them all the specialized gear that had evolved to meet Texas requirements, but the conditions up north led to changes.

For example, the various sorts of leather armor that were needed in the Texas thorns could be dispensed with in the northern grasslands. Leather chaps, essential in the south, could be left in the wagon when the herds cleared the brush country, as Rickey tells us. Tapaderos, the picturesque leather stirrup protectors used in Texas, were one of the first items to disappear from standard cowboy gear in the north country. Leather cuffs were not much needed in the north, but a lot of cowboys wore them anyway, perhaps as a matter of style.

Cowboy hats also underwent change as they moved north. It seems that in Texas, the slouch hat of the Confederacy and the sombrero from south of the border cross-bred and the offspring came north. Some of these descended models may have been a little more Southern, others a little more Mexican. According to Rickey, hats got a lot more standardized when they came to the northern plains. He says that most of the hats on the range were variants of the same model, the Stetson "Boss of the plains."

This model was available with different brim widths, in black or a light shade of gray, sometimes referred to as "white," and could be shaped to suit the wearer. Texans liked a broad brim and uncreased crown, Rickey says, while northern cowboys liked a creased crown and a narrower brim to resist the northern wind. Assuming that Rickey is right, that the cowboys in those old pictures are all wearing the same model hat, we can only be amazed at how differently they were shaped by the individuals.

Though the hats of the 1880s cowboy look familiar to us, the pants do not. The pants of that day, Rickey tells us, were likely to be wool, usually worn skin tight, with no belt or suspenders needed. Denim pants were in existence before 1880, but Rickey tells us that cowboys considered them "farmer pants" in the 1880s. This attitude changed as early as the 1890s and cowboys have worn Levi's up to the present. Other types of pants worn by cowboys of the era may have been leftover from a suit of town clothes, Rickey says. Indeed, cowboys' pants, jackets, and vests all were likely to be "leftover from a suit of town clothes." One suspects that one of his informants must have had a tendency to wear out his suits unevenly.

All of Rickey's living sources, old-timers who lived through the '80s on the range, made the point that flamboyance was not common in the dress of the cowboys. Everything was black or brown or gray, it seems, and flashiness was rare. Nevertheless, they mentioned that sometimes there was a fashion plate among them and that he could get away with it if he was a top hand. Otherwise, colorfully dressed cowpunchers were probably "coca-cola sokes," as cowboy artist Charlie Russell characterized some latter-day counterfeits. No coca-cola soke was E.C. "Teddy Blue" Abbott, who described one of his costumes in another book: a white Stetson hat that cost $10, a $12 pair of pants, and a good shirt and fancy boots with red and blue tops and a half moon and star on them. Those were the sort of clothes worn by a top hand, he said.

More than one hundred and ten years after Teddy Blue's day, modern cowboys sometimes turn back toward tradition. Many of the hats worn today look a lot more like those mutated sombreros of the 1880s than the flat-crowned, rolled brim models of the 1950s, for example.

Boots also show the retro fashion. Many of today's cowpunchers wear the knee-high "stovepipe" boot that is much more like the tall boots of the 1880s than the shorter models most commonly worn for the many years in between.

Rickey mentions two types of heels on old-time boots; a fairly high, square heel suitable for walking or riding, similar to those of the cavalry boots of the day, and a higher, undershot heel that has long been a point of separation between real cowboys and coca-cola sokes. The undershot heels are designed for one thing only, and that is riding.

A grounded cowboy trying to walk in these heels develops a peculiar roll to his gate, a little like a sailor who tends to roll with the waves even on dry ground. The message is: "I am a horseman, not a common pedestrian. Walking is not my thing." Unfortunately, Rickey treats the nature of the undershot heels lightly, and there is no illustration of them, so we don't know if the heels of the 1880s were like the heels of the 1990s. However, some of the boots in museums look very much like the ones worn these days by traditionalists who make a point of not walking too much.

The section of Rickey's book dealing with the coats worn by cowpunchers seems strangely deficient. For the most part, he concludes, cowboys didn't use coats. He says they made do with heavy wool shirts and sweaters worn under a slicker. No doubt this was true for the Texas men who came up the trail in the summer and went back home before winter set in, but those who stayed north over the winter probably could not have survived without a heavy coat. Rickey mentions several types of coats, the blanket coat favored by Canadians and trappers and the buffalo coat, but according to him, if a cowboy had even a jacket, it probably was a remnant from a suit of town clothes. If some cowboy did have a winter coat, Rickey said, it would be the cheapest sort available. Why this would be true, when these knights of the range didn't mind buying expensive gear of other types, is a mystery.

Strangely lacking a coat though he was said to be, the 1880s cowboy stranded in the north for the winter had warm gear for other portions of himself. For example, there were buckle-closed, rubber-bottomed, felt-top overshoes called Ar'tics, that could be traded from soldiers for whiskey. These boots in their various modifications over the years had a long run on the northern plains, worn in the coldest weather until the introduction of the felt-lined pac-type boots in recent decades.

Those 1880s cowboys wintering in the north could save their ears by wearing a Scotch cap—a woolen, billed cap with a pompon at the crest. The Scotch cap remains today much as it was in the 1880s, still seen on the range in the coldest weather.

One recurring theme in Rickey's book is the usefulness and availability of Army equipment to cowboys. It seems that the U.S. Army, cursed in every clime and era for always having the wrong equipment for the wrong time and place, got it right in the West of the 1880s. Besides felt overshoes, usable Army gear that cowboys could obtain in trade for whiskey included winter hats of muskrat fur, gray wool blankets that the cowboy could use in his bedroll or for a saddle blanket, blue army pants and shirts, and canteens—for the rare cowboy who wouldn't rather drink out of a cow track, Rickey suggests.

One oddity of Rickey's book is the amount of attention he gives to cowboy armaments. In a book of one hundred and thirty-three pages (in the original edition), pistols and holsters get eighteen pages. Rifles and carbines get nine pages, even though he says cowboys didn't have much use for a rifle. Perhaps he was thinking that arms were an especially important element of cowboy gear, and one that readers would be particularly interested in.

Rickey points out that the cowboys of the 1880s "gloried in the maximum exercise of personal freedom and individualism," and "the use of firearms to settle social misunderstandings was far more acceptable in the West of the 1880s than in more recent times."

Indeed, according to Rickey, the cowboy hardly felt dressed without his six-shooter somewhere about him. For going into town to take advantage of "social opportunity," Rickey writes, the cow-poke sometimes stuck his gun into a boot top or carried it out of sight in a waistband or shoulder holster. That way, a man was not conspicuously looking for trouble but was ready for it if it started.

Often the revolver was used with other than fatal intent, Rickey says. Harmless gunplay, such as keeping a tin can rolling, was a common form of entertainment. One of Rickey's sources said cowboys often spent more on cartridges than on clothes.

In our modern society where it is commonly accepted that "he who dies with the most toys wins," it is sobering to contemplate the sparsity of material goods that accompanied a cowboy through life. Outside of horse gear, about everything a man had in the way of personal effects was kept in a "warbag," a feed sack adapted for personal luggage. The contents of the warbag, Rickey tells us, were typically "something like two suits of underwear, a spare shirt, some socks, and a little loose personal stuff." Not much that would qualify as "toys."

Perhaps the nearest thing to a toy that a cowhand owned was his folding knife, Rickey tells us. Besides skinning ripe beeves that didn't winter and all the other typical uses, cowboys liked to use their knives, Rickey says (nothing about this in the movies), to play mumbletypeg, normally associated with kids in school yards.

As played by cowboys, this game consisted of competition to see who could do the most elaborate flips with a knife and get it to stick in the ground. Rickey gives us a clear illustration of a player setting up his move while others kibitz. Perhaps there was some wagering. As other writers have noted, the quality of a cowboy's goods often depended on how his luck had run recently in the various forms of gambling that he could not resist. There were range bosses who forbade their men to play mumbletypeg because it interfered with their work.

If a cowboy was fired, for excessive mumbletypeg play or other good reason, the boss would tell him to "Get your bed and clear out." Picking up one's bed was not burdensome to a cowboy. Rickey tells us a cowboy's bed consisted of piece of canvas about 18 feet long and six feet wide, doubled up from the bottom with the sides tucked under to contain whatever blankets or quilted "soogans" the man used. The warbag was also kept in the bed, and during the day the whole bed was rolled up into a tidy package and tied with a rope. One of the wagons that traveled with the drives was the "bed wagon," where the rolled beds were kept during the day. When a cowboy was unemployed and traveling on his own, the bed with all his personal gear inside was a light load for a packhorse.

Although Rickey's sources seem to have gone to great lengths to persuade him that there was very little that was fancy about a cowboy's equipment in the 1880s, Rickey notes a good deal of artistry in handmade gear. The quirt, for example, was often an example of fancy knots and braiding.

Similarly, according to Rickey, cowboys sometimes made their own horsehair bridles and fancied them up with geometric patterns in black and white hair, sometimes with reddish hair for color. Horsehair fancywork also was used in other ornamentation such as hatbands, Rickey writes. One-of-a-kind hatbands were only one way the cowboy of the 1880s gave individuality to his hat. The author says such handiwork was not done by many, but was always admired.

Authoritative though this book is, it is bound to conflict in some particulars with other sources. Rickey notes that "there will be areas for differences of opinion." One minor example, and I don't know of any major examples, is in the matter of bandanas. "In the eighties," Rickey writes, "nearly all bandanas were of cheap cotton. . . . Very few bandanas were of silk or linen, as such material was too costly."

Charley Russell would beg to differ. In *Good Medicine*, the book of his letters, Russell wrote: "I never knew a cowboy to wear anything [as a bandana] but silk" (first ed., 96). Ah well, if we could only gather up a dozen or so of those old timers, we could probably get that many opinions about anything. But they're all gone now, and all we have is the few sparse records they left, and the rare book such as Don Rickey's to tell us how it was. For Rickey's book, and for this fine reprint, we can be thankful.

Contents

*To the open-range cowboys,
named and unnamed, who passed
on information without which
this book could never have
been done.*

Introduction:
The 1880's Cowboy

The 1880's Cowboy

The open range cowboy has long been a bigger than life hero figure in American folklore and popular imagination. Like the frontier soldier of the western Indian Wars, his influence on the American mind has been far out of proportion to his numbers and the relatively short time span when the open range cattle industry spread north over the western plains from Texas after the Civil War. From 1865 to the middle 1880's the open range cattlemen reached their peak, and by 1900 they were fast disappearing, as homesteaders filed on choice lands, fenced the range and preempted the empire of grass that had been the open range cowboys' domain.

But what an appeal for easterners and Europeans wanting romance in dime novels and wild west shows — an appeal that has lasted undiminished into the 1970's, a century after the free grass cowboy became the symbol of romance and personal free-

dom and opportunity for personal mobility, adventure, and direct action that so many people feel they have lost or never knew. Perhaps our intense interest in the cowboy of the 1880's is akin to homesickness for a place we've never been and never was, and an image of ourselves as we wish we were.

The open range cowboy most often presented by the mass media since 1900 has usually been clothed, armed, and equipped in ways that certainly would have appeared strange to those who were cowboys in the eighties. Those leathery young old men the author knew twenty and more years ago, whose eyes glinted in recalling some long ago incident pointing up an example of what the times and experiences were really like to them; would frequently smile, snort and sarcastically put-down the picture of cowboys as depicted by movies and fiction writers.

The old raw-hiders are nearly all gone now, hopefully to a place where there are no fences, all the cattle are fat, camp cooks are kindly saints, and paydays come every week. Perhaps this account of the clothes they wore, the gear they used, the arms they carried, and the trappings and tools of their calling as they knew them will help to give a more accurate and sharply focussed picture of them as they were and of the life that they lived on the open range — before the fences went up, blooded cattle became the carefully tended standard of the beef industry, and a cow was still a rangy, mean slab-sided longhorn.

The open range era was a frontier phase of the economic development of the great plains, and as was true of nearly all frontier life, that of the 1880's cowboy was marked by a general lack of show and ostentation. Life on the range and with the trail herds was rough and crude. Clothing, tools, arms, and equipments were purely functional, and usually the cheapest that could be had consistent with the utility for which the various articles were needed. The colorfully dressed cowboy of popular legend was a later development, in times when goods could be secured much more cheaply than in the frontier years and the cowboy had become a romantic American hero type. The attitude of the 1880's cowman was one of make-do born of necessity — to get along with as little as possible, combined with a sort of prideful self denial coupled to fierce individualism showing personal style and preference. The cowboy wanted to make damn certain he wasn't mistaken for anything other than what he was! Disdainful of laborers, soldiers, townsmen, and especially "sodbuster" farmers; he wanted to be sure that no one could mistake him for such lesser folk. His speech, manners and dress were ways he could insure that he projected the image he wanted — a working cowboy. As a rule, he was leery of anything fancy; but there were a few vain "shadow watchers" and "mail-order" cowboys. Such fashion plates often assumed a heavier load though, as such showiness imposed the need to be real top hands if they were to be accepted by their comrades. The open range cowboy more likely prided himself on endurance and skills, especially physical dexterity with a rope, gun, branding iron, knife; and in wrestling, running, jumping and above all riding. Many were careful craftsmen in braiding horse hair and rawhide and a good hand was expected to be able to turn his hand to any acceptable work.

He was often a very competitive sort of cuss; an attitude that showed itself in riding, shooting, knife throwing, roping, drinking, brand reading, dancing, and singing. Like a plains Indian, the old time range cowboy often "owned" his own songs. He was nearly always young, generally light on cash and long on hope and as independent as the wild longhorns he herded.

The most predominant single influence on the dress and equipments of open range cowboys in the 1880's was the fact that a great many of them had come from Texas with the trail herds, bringing with them styles of dress, weapons, horse gear and equipments they had known in Texas. On the central and northern ranges, some of these items were discarded or modified to fit the somewhat changed conditions, but the Texas influence remained predominant throughout the era of the open range. There were some who were fashion leaders of a kind, but most were not very

style conscious. None had much money, and as 1880's trail driver Ben Bird observed, "some spent more for cartridges than they did for clothes". Of course, economics had much to do with how well a cowboy was dressed, and often a rancher or foreman would be better dressed and sit a better saddle than did the average cowboy; however most cowboys were very quality conscious when it came to clothing and equipment, and though not very colorful in appearance their fixings were often durable and of good quality.

Many cowboys came from frontier communities and wore clothing made for them by their women folk, or bought such rough home-made clothing from stores that had taken it in barter. Clothing usually was dark-hued; brown, grey or blue, sometimes black. Fast dyes for bright colors had not yet been introduced, and dark clothes did not show dirt so quickly. The bandana was often the only touch of color about the 1880's cowboy. All the old time open range cowboys stressed the fact they had had very little money to spend on clothing in a time when a good hand drew from thirty to forty dollars a month. As a rule, a cowboy was lucky to have a set of clean clothes when he got to town, much less own a special outfit for the occasion.

All the cowboy's clothing and possessions had to be carried with him on his horse or in his bedroll. Each article had to serve a useful function, or as in the case of his hat, several functions.

His clothes, arms, tools and trappings had to stand a great deal of rough use; as he was usually out where replacements could not be obtained or easily afforded. Bearing in mind the cowboy personality and living conditions in the 1880's, each item of his dress, arms, tools and horse gear will be described and explained to help us see the open range cowboy as he really was during the years when he ranged the western plains, from the Rio Grande to the Canadian border.

Cowboy Clothing

Hats

The hat was usually a cowboy's most easily identifying trademark. No single item of apparel so quickly identified him for what he was as did the cowboy hat. This hat seems to have evolved in about 1870 from the earlier slouch hat popular on the frontier and in the South, and the wide-brimmed, high-crowned Mexican sombrero.

The John B. Stetson Company marketed a specially designed cowboy hat in the early 1870's. This hat, known as the "boss of the plains", was made in various brim widths, generally from two and a half to slightly over four inches, with a crown seven inches high. On the northern ranges the brim was usually a little narrower than in Texas, about three and a half inches. The hat came in two colors, black and white; although the white was actually more of a grey shade. It remained pretty well standard with cowboys for many years, as it served their needs perfectly and was noted for

holding its shape well despite frequent wettings and much abuse. Most 1880's cowboys added a chin string to hold the hat on in high winds. Some favored looping this string around the back of the head, and some wore it under the chin.

Having most likely come up from Texas, many cowboys wore the Mexican straw sombrero in summer, with its very broad brim to ward off sun and high, peaked crown to keep the wearer's head cool. Stiff brimmed hats were almost never worn by cowboys of the eighties, and were more commonly associated with surveyors, engineers, and miners.

Hat crowns were sometimes dented and creased and sometimes left round. Texans generally left their hat crowns uncreased and round. A special hat band was often added. These bands were of leather, snakeskin, or braided horsehair; usually made by the wearer, not only for ornament, but to help the hat keep its shape when wet. The hat band was generally from one half to three quarters of an inch wide. If made of leather, the band was commonly fastened by a small silver or nickle buckle, and sometimes was ornamented all round with tacks or small conchos. Many hat bands were of braided horsehair; perhaps in black, with white or red hair interwoven in geometric patterns. Making horsehair hat bands and novelties, such as wristlets, watch chains, headstalls and bridles was a fairly popular cowboy pastime. In time, the art

17

of braiding and knot-working horsehair was taught in the Montana penitentiary at Deer Lodge, and the manufacture of horsehair objects by someone was quite likely to provoke joking comments as to where the craftsman had "learned his trade" and what "college" he had graduated from.

The cowboy's hat was wide-brimmed to protect him from the blazing sun of summer and from all kinds of bad weather. The high crown allowed enough air space to keep the wearer's head moderately cool. Aside from head cover, it was used to carry water, to signal, to haze stock with, and perhaps to fan a campfire to life. It was almost indispensible, and could cost up to $20.00; a big part of a thirty dollar a month cowboy's pay. In the winter, a scarf or strip of flannel cloth was often tied around the hat and under the wearer's chin to protect his face and ears when out in "northers" and driving sleet or snow.

A few cowboys acquired other types of headgear for winter. Some had seal or muskrat fur caps, but these were not common. Most such hats were secured from soldiers, as muskrat hats became standard winter issue in the 1880's. Soldiers were often not averse to trading these hats, as well as other articles of clothing, for money or whiskey, as Shy Ousterhout recalled from his own experiences on the western Dakota range. Sometimes, a cowboy might have a woolen cloth winter hat, commonly known as a

Hats
(A) A strip of flannel over a Stetson kept the ears and face from freezing.
(B) The wool Scotch cap has been a favorite for almost a hundred years. The ear band folds up inside.
(C) Muskrat caps had flaps to let down over the ears and a bill flap in front to protect the face when folded out. Lots of these Army caps found their way into other hands.
(D) Mexican style with tie in back.
(E) Stetson with tie and plain leather hat band.
(F) Hat with horse hair hat band.

Scotch cap. They had a somewhat square shape on top, with a button on the top of the crown, a peak of the same material as the cap, and a wide flap that could be turned down to cover the back of the head and the ears. Such winter hats are still popular in many parts of the West.

Coats and Jackets

Because of the near universal use of the water-proof pommel slicker and the common wearing of vests, many cowboys did not even own a coat or jacket. But, as 1880's cowboy and horse wrangler Jake Tomamichel explained, they "usually went shirt-sleeved". Some variety did exist among jackets when they were worn though. In the South, and among those who had come up the trails from Texas, a hip or waist length canvas or buckskin jacket was popular with fellows who had brush-popped wild cattle in Texas, where protection from brush and mesquite thorns was the main reason for wearing one. However, very few of these jackets were ornamented in any way, except for possibly a little fringing. They usually showed a degree of Mexican influence in the small lapels and "charo" tailoring, but were otherwise quite plain.

If a cowboy on the northern range owned a sack coat, it was almost certain to be left over from his having sometime bought a

(A) Laced leather vests were especially popular in Texas.
(B) Common suit or "sack" coats were owned by many cowboys.
(C) Cardigan sweaters were warm and yet allowed a lot of freedom — jersey pull-overs were also common.

ready-made suit in town. It was generally an old wool garment that had once upon a time come with a suit of "town clothes".

Some types of coats did become popular with a few cowboys though, such as the "sweetor" wide-waled corduroy coats that came in about 1890. These coats were never common though, and the make-do ethic of the open range cowboy was more likely than not to influence him to not even own a coat. If he did own one, it was almost certain to be black or some other dark color; somewhat the worse for wear, and bearing plain evidence of having been rolled or bunched up in a "warbag" or bedroll.

Besides vests and slickers, many cowboys wore wool sweaters in cold weather. A sweater was not nearly so restrictive of movement as a coat. Most sweaters were of the jersey type, or if home-made of the turtle-neck variety. Jake Tomamichel fondly recalled the 1885 gift of a jersey sweater to him by some older cowboys he wrangled horses for as a kid run-away from Ft. Laramie. "Later, when I understood what was going on", mused Jake, "I was certain they were horse-thieves who had me herding for them while they were gone, but that was the finest Christmas present I ever remember". Like other clothing of the eighties, all sweaters were dark; usually grey or black.

Shirts

Cowboy shirts of the 1880's were a far cry from the colorful, snuggly tailored garments of recent years. Since many of them came from the frontier regions of Texas, a large number wore home-made shirts; quite often the hickory shirt with a checked pattern, according to Ben Bird, who trailed his first herd to the northern range country in 1881. Such shirts had straight sleeves and small turned down collars. Contrary to some movies and romanticized artist conceptions, little evidence seems to indicate the wearing of the "fireman's" or miner's type shirts, with a row of buttons down each side to secure the chest protector. Only a few of these were worn. Most shirts had buttons only part way down the front, usually three, or perhaps laces instead. These were all pull-over shirts.

Store-bought shirts were loose fitting, like the home variety, pull-over and with loose hung straight sleeves and close fitting

cuffs. Colors were usually dark, grey, blue, or black being very popular. Because shirts were not ready-made in a wide variety of sizes and sleeve lengths, many cowboys wore arm garters to adjust the length of the sleeves. Most shirts had but one pocket in those days, if any.

As the cowboy usually went without a coat, his shirt was often an outer garment. Wool shirts were popular, because they were warm and would absorb sweat. Many shirts were made of dark colored flannel. Army shirts of the 1880's were of tightly woven wool twill in navy blue, and were popular with cowboys. These shirts could be had through trade with soldiers, and sometimes from post traders at military establishments. Like other shirts of the eighties, it was a pull-over type, with buttons from the collar to about four inches from the belt line.

One of the most popular commercial shirts was a common pull-over made of a black material very much like modern sateen. This material wore very well, and above all did not show the dirt. Washing clothes in a water hole, with mud for soap, did not make for much in looks if the garments were colors that were not already very dark. In later times, the railroad hobo used the same kind of "thousand mile shirt", for the same reason the cowboys did.

Some striped shirts were worn by 1880's cowboys, and especially those made of silk. Though quite costly, silk shirts were long

All shirts were pull-over, and not close fitting. They had to be warm and turn the wind — nearly all were dark colored.

wearing and popular because they were closely woven and would turn the wind. Jake Tomamichel and Shy Ousterhout remarked that they always tried to have a striped silk shirt. Like other shirts of the times, the sleeves were full and baggy, the body was loose, and the cuffs were snug. For special occasions, a cowboy might have donned a white shirt, but he certainly did not work in or habitually wear one.

Bandanas

In the 1880's, a bandana was often the only touch of color in a cowboy's dress, and like the hat was a feature that served to distinguish the range rider from other folk. In summer it absorbed sweat and in winter it served the purpose of a muffler. Tied around the face it gave protection from dust and bitter winter winds. In a pinch it could serve as a tourniquet or bandage. Bandanas were virtually universal among southern range cowmen, but since dust was not much of a problem in the north, not all cowboys wore them there.

The origin of the word bandana comes from India, where it refers to a method of dying cotton cloth. By folding the cloth in a special way before dipping it in the dye, a figured pattern could be dyed into cotton. In the eighties, nearly all bandanas were of cheap cotton; usually with a pattern but sometimes in solid colors. Very few bandanas were of silk or linen, as such material was too

A

B

C

D

E

F

Dale Crawford '76

costly for the use the cowboy wanted. As worn by cowboys, the bandana was usually tied loosely around the throat. A few men made loop rings for them of horsehair or bone. Long woollen mufflers were common in winter, and many cowboys used a long strip of flannel in place of a muffler or bandana.

The Bandana had many uses:
(A) To keep out the trail dust in summer and the cold in winter.
(B) Used as a sling.
(C) To cover the back of his neck from the sun.
(D) As a towel when he got a chance to clean off the trail dust.
(E) To wrap a cut or wound.
(F) To signal someone far away.

Trousers

Although Levi Strauss had introduced his style of heavy denim pants before 1880, close fitting woolen pants were by far the most popular with cowboys, and were the trousers most often worn by them in the eighties. Another very common type of pants among cattlemen were the brown "jeans". These were mostly home-made garments, tailored for a snug fit, of brown duck or twill material, as recalled by Ben Bird. Of course, a good many cowboys also wore trousers that were left over from a suit of "town-clothes", usually in black or some other dark color.

Trousers in the 1880's were cut differently than in recent times, and the cowboy had reasons for his preferences. Close fitting pants did not ride up on the wearer, and the leg was made so as to fit snuggly from the hips down. Pockets were across the front, at a slight downward angle toward the hip, rather than along the outer seam; because objects carried in outseam pockets had a way of

Army pants were good quality, hard finished wool — and cheap.

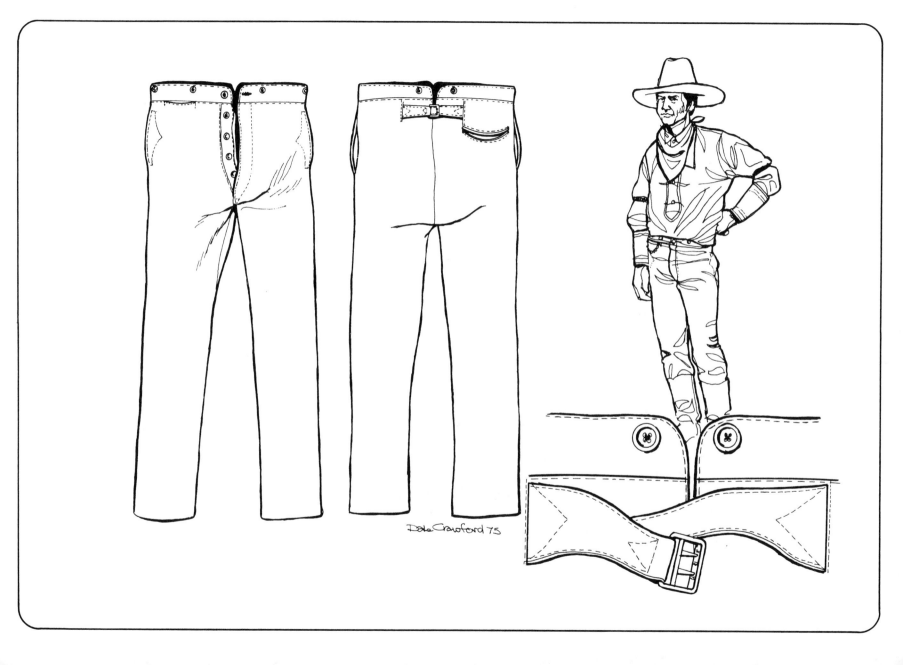

Dale Crawford 75

working up and out of the pocket when riding. Pants material was often a dark, narrow striped variety called "gamblers stripe", as worn by 1800's cowboys Sam Hotchkiss and Ben Bird. Because these pants were built to a snug fit, many men wore neither belt nor "galluses".

Since cowboys traded with soldiers for other items of clothing, they also did so for the light blue wool army pants. These pants were quite popular, as they were made of a heavy grade tightly woven wool material known as kersey. They were cut to fit closely around the waist and down the leg. To insure a snug fit around the waist, they had an adjustable band attached in the back, held at the desired tension by a small buckle.

The most distinctive type of cowboy trousers were the "California pants" that became especially popular in the late 1880's and early 1890's, and were designed for the cattlemen. These pants were cut very close in the leg and fit almost skin tight all around. When the open range cow outfits came out of the disastrous winter of 1886-87, one cowman, who had been very successful, remarked that all he had in the outcome was a pair of high-heeled boots, the striped pants, and about $4.80 worth of clothes. "California pants" were most often striped, but some had a thin dark plaid design over a lighter buckskin color. They cost about $7.50 per pair, and as Teddy Blue Abbott put it, "were about the best pants ever made to ride in''.

As mentioned before, blue denim ''Levi'' trousers were not favored by 1880's cowboys. They were considered poor man's wear, or more likely the sort of clothes a ''pilgrim'' farmer would wear. Those cowboys who did wear such pants did so only when they hadn't the price of any other kind. Strange to say, this attitude changed radically in the 1890's, and ''Levis'' became quite popular with cowboys for rough work. In the eighties some few cowboys sported buckskin pants, especially those in Texas and on the southern range.

If worn at all, most younger men favored a plain leather belt, though quite a few wore ''galluses''. Most trousers fit close enough so that neither belt nor suspenders were really necessary. In the matter of wearing style for trousers, eighties cowmen were about evenly divided as to wearing 'em outside or stuffed into boot tops.

Toward the end of the eighties, wide-waled ''sweetor'' corduroy pants became fairly popular on the northern range. This was the same material that some coats were made of. By the late 1890's this type of corduroy pants had pretty well passed from the scene. Though the material was very durable, the build of these pants was not much for strong, explained Shy Ousterhout, and it was a saying of the times that a fellow who bought a pair of ''sweetor'' pants had better get him a spool of tough linen thread and re-sew all the seams so they wouldn't pull out on him.

Vests

Like the high crowned wide-brimmed Stetson and the bandana, the wearing of a vest as an outer garment has been generally associated with the cowboys of the open range years. This concept is pretty well rooted in fact, as many cowboys did wear them; especially in Texas, where many central and northern range cowmen came from. Since the shirts of the time usually had but one pocket, if any, and the close fitting trousers of the 1880's cowboy made the carrying of articles in the pockets uncomfortable, many cowboys wore a vest simply because of the four pockets it afforded for carrying smaller personal possessions. As an outer garment, the vest allowed greater freedom of movement than a coat or jacket, and the factor of style also had an influence, as the wearing of a vest was considered stylish. Very often, the vest was a leftover from a suit of town clothes, but as Shy Ousterhout and ex-buffalo hunter and 1880's cowboy Harry Schlosher commented,

Lots of arm freedom was needed working on horseback — the sleeveless vest allowed this and was also warm. Its pockets held a lot of small things too.

storekeepers who catered to cowboy trade sometimes bought consignments of vests from large clothing companies.

Most vests were not fancy though, and like the other parts of an eighties cowman's outfit were usually black or in some dark color, perhaps with some figure in the material. Vests of spotted antelope or deer skin were all the thing with a few Texas men according to Ben Bird, who recalled that some of the younger cowboy trail drivers of the 1880's favored such a vest, if they could obtain one. Harvey Robinson and Shy Ousterhout mentioned that there were many cowboys on the northern range who didn't wear a vest, and only wore a heavy wool shirt as an outer garment in place of either a coat or vest. By the 1890's the calf-skin vest had begun to achieve some popularity, but not so in the 1880's.

Outer Coats, Slickers and Overcoats

Except for some line-riding late in the eighties and a little odd-job work around ranch headquarters, there was little employment for an open range cowboy in winter. Many Texans, who had trailed herds north to stock the range there, or to army posts and Indian reservations on beef contracts, drifted back south with the approach of winter. Since many of these cowmen did not stay through the bitter winters of the northern ranges, many did not even own an outer coat or heavy overcoat. Those who did winter-over, often had the cheapest possible type of overcoat. Shy Ouster-hout pointed out that only a prosperous rancher could afford the luxury of a heavy raccoon skin coat that cost about $50.00.

Some blanket coats were worn by northern cowboys, but not many, as they had been designed for timbered country and were not warm enough for the cutting winds of the plains. Some of these blanket coats were colorful though; mostly white, with broad bands of red, blue and orange. Lack of money kept some cowboys from owning on overcoat, and Jake Tomamichel recalled wintering at one outfit where "there was one overcoat in the whole outfit, and it was loaned around to his friends by the owner".

For those cowboys who did own a winter coat, the most common kind was what was known as a "sourdough coat". This was about the same length as a suit-coat or mackinaw, but made of canvas or duck; often painted to make it wind and water-proof. For warmth, these coats were lined with blanketing or heavy flannel; Shy Ousterhout recalled that cowboys brought such coats to his mother, to have them relined.

Only a very few cowboys of the 1880's had buffalo or fur coats. They were too heavy and bulky for riding and for carrying around in a bedroll. A few did obtain buffalo coats though, mostly through swapping liquor to soldiers. Most buffalo coats were almost ankle length, with a collar that could be turned up to about eye-level. The one in my collection weighs sixteen pounds and most probably was acquired from a soldier during the 1890 Sioux campaign. Some such coats had buttons, but most, like this one, were double-breasted, with toggle fasteners and wool wristlets inside the sleeves.

(A) A canvas coat with blanket lining was good cover in winter.

(B) Blanket coats were associated with the far north and French-Indian half-breeds, but some cowboys used 'em. The Hudson's Bay Co. still sells the blankets they were made from.

(C) Yellow slicker, to keep out rain and weather, covered the rider and saddle on horseback.

(D) Buffalo coats were owned by some, but not many — they were warm and not easy to move around in.

A

B

C

D

Mostly, we've talked about kinds of outer coats for winter that few cowboys made use of in the 1880's. Since the nature of their calling compelled cowboys to be out in all kinds of weather, the question could fairly be, well, what did they wear to protect themselves from cold? For a great many, the answer was that with a heavy shirt, vest and possibly an old suit coat, a cowboy could keep fairly warm by adding the near universally owned water-proof pommel slicker. Ben Bird observed that this could keep a rider warm in all but the bitterest weather.

Of all the outer garments worn by 1880's cowboys, none was so common as the yellow pommel slicker of light canvas or duck, water-proofed with linseed oil. The pommel slicker was introduced just before 1880, especially for the cowboy trade. It fell almost to the ankle, and was made to entirely cover the wearer and the saddle while riding. The wide skirts of this raincoat came forward to cover the rider's legs in wet and cold weather, and painted with linseed oil it was pretty well wind and water-proof.

The yellow slicker was generally known as a "Fishbrand", or "Tower" slicker from the name and trademarks of the firm that supplied most of them. When not in use, slickers were usually carried rolled inside out, tied to the back of the saddle or cantle. Slickers had to stand much abuse and still retain their water-proof quality. They were often used to beat out grass fires. In the

1880's, a yellow slicker cost the cowboy about $3.50. They had metal buttons, often with the word "Tower" on them. Before about 1910, the collar was usually lined with red flannel; after that the lining was commonly an olive drab material. There were a few black slickers in use, but not many, as Ben Bird and Shy Ousterhout cautioned that a black slicker seemed to spook horses easier and was quite stiff in cold weather due to the paint that had been added to the linseed oil. The fact is, the yellow pommel slicker has changed very little in over ninety years.

Gloves

Most 1880's cowboys wore wrist length gloves the year round. These gloves were nearly always made of buckskin, and almost never ornamented in any way. Very, very few cowboys of that time wore the gauntlet type glove. Ben Bird explained that such bucket tops could cause a serious accident when roping, and all kinds of stuff would get caught in them. Some gauntlets became popular in the 1890's, but were never much used by real working cowboys.

Buckskin gloves were often purchased at a store in town. In Medora, North Dakota, an ex-soldier named Schyler LeBo hunted and trapped for a living, and in the winter made buckskin gloves to sell to cowboys. In winter, many northern range cowboys wore buckskin mittens lined with wool or fur.

"A man can always get new gloves, but he's only got one pair of grabbers to last him through."

Rope burns could put a cowboy out of action — buckskin gloves were good insurance.

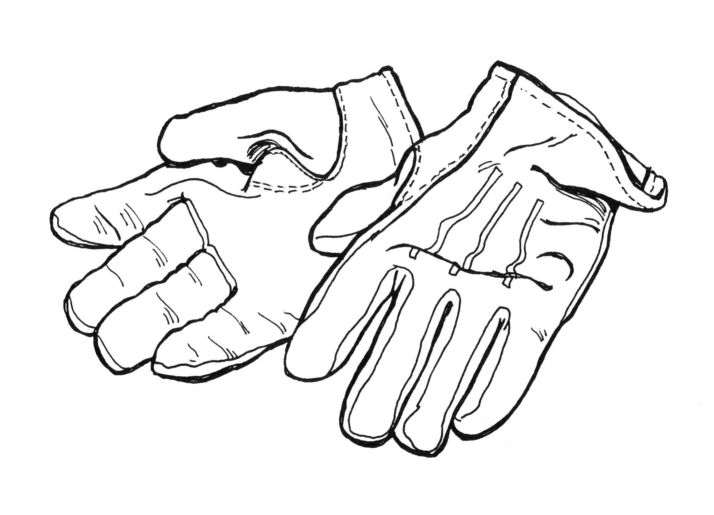

Chaps

Chaps originated, as loose leather leg protectors called "chap-areras", in Mexico. By the time the northern ranges opened up for stocking with Texas longhorns after the Sioux Wars were over in the late 1870's, most Texas cowboys wore them as the open range cattle empire spread north. Chaps became popular in the south because of the protection they offered against the rough scrub and mesquite brush. Shy Ousterhout emphasized that almost every Texas cowboy had a pair of chaps when he arrived in the north. They weren't worn quite so much in the north though, and their most common use was an extra covering when riding at night or in cold and wet weather. During the day, they were usually wrapped in the bedroll or thrown in the bed wagon.

Almost all 1880's chaps were of tough but supple leather. No fur or Angora chaps, such as were to become popular in the range country west of the Rocky Mountains, seem to have been worn

Shotgun chaps, for protection from brush and weather.

on the great plains until about 1887. Even then they were rare, and likely to be the property of a cowman trailing cattle east to the northern plains from Idaho and Oregon. The common chaps of the eighties cowboy were the closed leg variety, explained Ben Bird, "like a pair of straight leg trousers with the seat cut out". These straight cut legs were usually thonged together along the outer edge of the leg in a style known as "shotgun chaps". A short fringe was sometimes cut along the thonged seam, and occasionally a cowboy would ornament his chaps with silver conchos, or perhaps Mexican pesos with holes punched through them and laced to the edge of the chaps legs. Other conchos or pesos were sometimes spaced along the belt, which was integral with the chaps — perhaps three on each side. A patch pocket was frequently laced or sewn on at the top of each leg, four or five inches from the top of the belt. The wide bat-wing chaps did not come into use until much later, after the open range years were over.

Boots

Cowboy boots of the 1880's were very similar in shape and form to those made in recent years; the main difference was that the boots of the eighties came up much higher on the leg, reaching almost to the knee, and the toe was more rounded than pointed. No fancy leathers were used, and very few showed any ornamentation. The usual forward sloping heel was about two inches high, but some boots were made with a square heel, like cavalry boots. Nearly all boots were made of black leather; "French calf" being especially favored according to Ben Bird and Shy Ousterhout. Ornamentation, if any, was limited to a little fancy stitching on the boot tops, but this was not common in the 1880's.

Most boots had a pair of leather pull-on straps sewn into the inside of the boot on each side at the top, so that they extended above the tops for an inch or so. Harvey Robinson and Jake Tomamichel observed that flashy "mule ear" straps, flopping over the

boot tops for several inches, were not common and pretty certainly marked their wearer as a "dude" or green-horn newcomer to the range country.

Some cowboys had their boots made-to-order, but many bought theirs ready-made. Most boots were made in small shops catering to cowboy trade. Pegged boots, in which the foot portion was secured to the sole with hardwood pegs, cost a few dollars more than sewn boots. Prices for boots varied from about $7.00 for ready-mades to $15.00 for made-to-measure boots. A cowboy could spend as much as he wanted on his boots, but very few seem to have felt the need to invest a great deal of money in their footwear. Extra long heels were stylish with those who did order more expensive boots.

As with other items of cowboy clothing in the eighties, many of the socks worn were home-made articles. Women in the frontier communities frequently knit cotton string and woolen yarn socks to exchange at a store for commercial goods. Cowboys bought these socks from the storekeepers and itinerant "huckster wagons". The "huckster wagon" man was the old time pack peddlar of earlier American acquaintance in the East and midwestern regions tricked out with a wagon and team to enable him to travel from ranch to ranch with a sort of wheel-borne general store of clothes, hardware, sundries, and all the items cattle people either had a yen or a use for. In the northern range country, some cowboys bought "Dutch socks" from the huckster, or from a store in town, for winter warmth. These socks were almost knee-high and double knit of heavy wool.

In winter, many cowboys in the north wore rubber and felt overshoes or "ar'tics", and many of those were traded from soldiers. "Ar'tics" were rubber soled, with black felt uppers fastened with metal clasps across the front.

Spurs

A pretty fair variety of spurs were used by 1880's cowboys. Some were made by local blacksmiths and some were bought from commercial sources. With Texans, the heavier Mexican influence was evident in the usually more massive and sometimes ornamented spurs they wore. Since a great many open range cowmen had drifted north, trailing herds to and beyond the British line, a large percentage of the spurs seen all over the great plains country were these large heavy iron spurs.

Texas spurs usually had long-pronged rowels, up to two inches in diameter. Ben Bird recalled making rowels for his spurs by punching a hole through the center of a Mexican silver peso, then filing teeth all around it. Sam Hotchkiss' Texas spurs had small metal "jinglers" hung from the end of the spur shank in such a way as to make the rowels hit them when they turned. Some spurs had other small pieces of metal, called "clinkers", dangling from

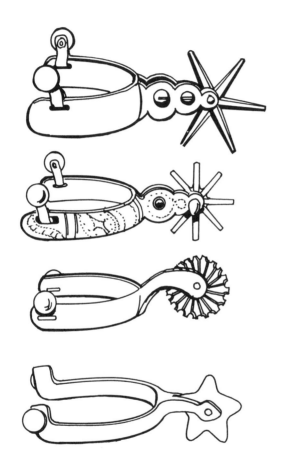
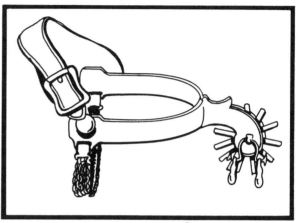

Dale Crawford 76

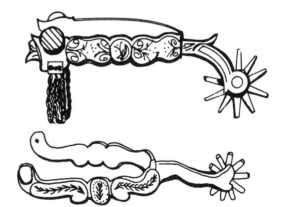

the shank itself. On the northern range, many cowboys favored smaller rowels for their spurs; about one and a half inch diameters, on a two inch shank.

Spurs were among the first items of cowboy dress that were beginning to show some ornamentation in the 1880's. Silver inlays on spurs, as well as those of brass and copper, were becoming stylish among working cowboys. Jake Tonamichel still had a handsome pair of spurs with a goosehead fashioned at the end of the gooseneck shank. They were made of iron, with small silver inlays on the shanks. The two most popular types were the "Cross L", a large heavy spur; and the "O.K.", a lighter and smaller sort of spur that didn't drag so much.

Cuffs

Leather cuffs, to protect the cowboy's forearms in rough brush country and from rope burns, seem to have originated in Texas. Ben Bird recalled that when he made his first trail drive north from Texas in 1881, "all the men wore leather cuffs for brush riding". Quite a few cowboys on the central and northern ranges wore cuffs in the 1880's as well. Cuffs were usually about eight inches long, sometimes with a band of stamped design in the leather at each end. Some few cuffs had a row or two of silver or nickle studs set into them, but such fanciness was not common in the eighties, said Jake Tonamichel and Shy Ousterhout. Cuffs usually fastened with a snap at the large end, and had a leather strap and small white metal buckle to close them at the wrist.

Cuffs seem to have been widely used up to about 1910, but for some reasons rapidly lost popularity after 1900. Not all northern range cowboys of the 1880's wore cuffs, but many who had come up from Texas did.

Russet and brown leather cuffs protected against rope burns and brush — many were plainer than these.

Underwear

Range riding and trail driving compelled the cowman to be out in all kinds of weather; he needed a heavy type of underwear. Most underwear in the eighties was of the one piece union-suit type, of the wrist and ankle length persuasion. It was usually of cotton flannel or wool, though silk underwear was sometimes worn in winter, when he could afford it, said Ben Bird. Most underwear was grayish white, or sometimes red. Occasionally, underwear came in a two piece suit, also wrist and ankle length.

"Long-johns" were cowboy pajamas — the quilted "soogans" were warm — and cheap.

Arms and Equipment

Revolvers

Almost every cowpuncher in the 1880's wore a heavy calibre revolver on a combination gun and cartridge belt; except perhaps when in town, but most certainly on trail drives when all his earthly possessions went with him. Although the Army had pretty well surpressed Indian warfare on the northern ranges by the eighties, it was still prudent for cowboys to be on their guard against small groups of wandering warriors whose feelings were sometimes pretty hostile, if the occasion for venting them came up in isolated situations. Harry Schlosher remarked that in country close to or on eastern Montana Indian reservations, cowboys made it a practice to ride two or three together rather than alone; as it was not smart to offer temptation to a buck whose heart might be bad. Then too, a firm framework of law and order had not been effectively established, and there were more than a few range riders whose business wasn't on the square, or who had left some other climate for reasons of health that had more to do with law officers than medical opinion. Recalling his early years on the northern range, Jake Tonamichel commented that "the country was full of Texas gunmen in the eighties".

It should also be kept in mind that personal recourse to arms and the use of firearms for settling social misunderstandings was far more acceptable in the West of the 1880's than in more recent times. Carry-overs from earlier frontier attitudes towards the carrying and use of firearms are still present in the American mind, and were even more so in the eighties and among a brand of men who gloried in the maximum exercise of personal freedom and individualism.

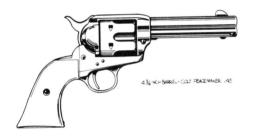

4¾ INCH BARREL - COLT PEACEMAKER .45

The revolver was the open range cowboy's prime self-defense weapon, but it had other uses as well. It was handy for signalling, for killing wolves and coyotes, for hunting game for the pot, and was not infrequently a source of sport and amusement. Such amusement sometimes got a little out of hand, as smoking up a town in a spirit of bravado was a little irksome to the law and order folks. In *Good Medicine,* one of Charley Russell's pencil sketches recorded just such an incident, when "Nolen Armstrong was bush-whacked at Culbertson while smoking up the town by the deputy sheriff".

In revolver shooting, the cowboy was most often a snap shot

rather than a deliberate shooter. Some cowboys practiced a great deal, but others could not afford to buy extra ammunition. A great many saved their shell cases and reloaded them to while away bunkhouse hours, as cartridges were quite expensive. Competitive and trick shooting was fairly popular in the 1880's. Shooting at tin cans thrown in the air, or keeping a can rolling on the ground by hitting it with bullets were common forms of amusement shooting. One type of competition shooting that was especially favored by Texas cowboys was to rapid fire the contents of a revolver at a post, while riding a horse at full gallop. The winner was the man who placed the most shots in the post, closest together. Ben Bird estimated that about one third of the cowboys of the eighties were what could be termed really good shots.

For distance shooting, and when accuracy was most wanted, the revolver was usually held with both hands, straight in front of the shooter's body. This was the hold most often used in hunting.

Nearly all cowboys carried their revolver in a large loop-through, open top holster hung on a cartridge belt. Only a fool put more than five cartridges in a six-shot revolver cylinder, unless he were expecting some fast and serious action. In normal use, the hammer was let down on the empty chamber, as a safety precaution. A fall with a revolver whose hammer was resting on the safety notch over a live shell could be disastrous, as the safety notch on a .45 or .44 Colt was fairly brittle and easily broken, allowing the hammer to strike the cartridge primer setting it off. When going into town, the gun belt was often left at the ranch, or in his bed-roll on a trail drive. If such was the case, the revolver was carried tucked into the belly-band of the trousers, under a suit coat, or perhaps carried in an out-of-sight shoulder holster. Shoulder holsters were most commonly used in winter though, so the revolver could be more easily reached under a slicker or outer coat.

Ben Bird recalled an instance where two men had bad blood with a third fellow and schemed to provoke him into a set-up gun fight. One of the two plotters loosened the hammer spring on the third man's revolver when he saw it laying on the man's bunk while its owner was washing up outside. The gun with its loose hammer spring was put back in its holster, the owner came in, buckled it on, and then dressed to go line riding on that cold fall morning. The two schemers stopped outside and began to harass the third man. Words went back and forth, and the chief schemer drew his gun. But before he could get a shot off, the third fellow drew and fired another gun from a shoulder holster the plotters hadn't known about.

While most cowboys were peaceably inclined fellows, there

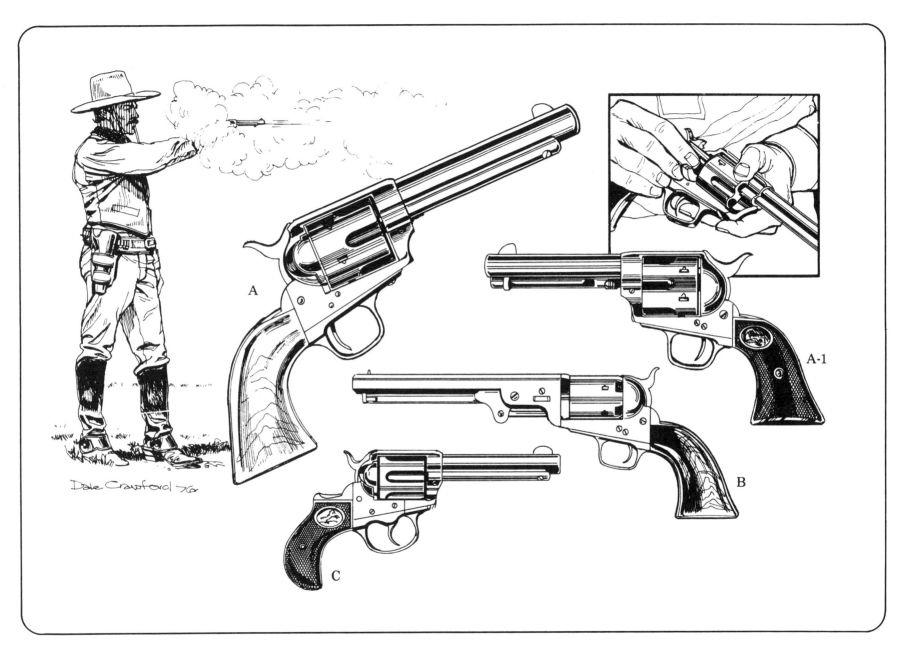

Dale Crawford 76

A

A-1

B

C

Colts

(A) "Peacemaker", .45 calibre, of the 1870's, with one-piece wood grip — after 1882 grips were two-piece, of moulded rubber, like those on (A-1).

(B) 1851, .36 calibre cap-and-ball loading "navy" model, popular before the 1870's — its frame and grips were used on the 1872 and later "Peacemaker" metallic cartridge revolvers.

(C) Double-action, 1877 "Lightning", came in .38 and .41 calibres, and were used to some extent by cowmen.

All cartridge Colts loaded and emptied shells through a side-gate until after 1892. Their heavy lead bullets hit very hard and made deadly wounds.

were a few who were on the prod or on the dodge. A few of these were professional gunmen, who occasionally worked as cowboys. Some of these types might have a special leather lining sewn in the back pocket of their pants, and carried their revolver in this leather pocket when in town.

Of all the various types and makes of revolvers on the market in the 1880's, the single action Colt, model 1872 "Army" or "Peacemaker" was by far the most popular revolver on the open range. Basically, this was the 1872 Army revolver, usually with some slight modifications. Production of this revolver continued until 1940, with very few changes, until production needs for arms orders for the allies caused suspension of the single action Colt. So popular has this weapon become, and so much a part of the western tradition, that the Colt firm resumed production in 1956.

Civilian purchasers of the single action Colt could order it in a variety of barrel lengths other than the seven and one half inch Cavalry style used by the Army. It could also be ordered in a variety of external finishes, with or without engraving, with special grips, and in an assortment of calibres other than the .45 Army calibre.

Most popular with the cowboys of the 1880's were the .45, .44, .41, and especially the .44/.40 calibre Colts, according to Ben Bird and Harry Schlosher. The .45 was the heaviest, and was the standard Army revolver cartridge until after 1892. The .44/40 cartridge was the same ammunition as was used in the model 1873 Winchester rifle and carbine, giving the advantage of interchangeability of shells for revolver and saddle-gun. Colts were also chambered for other Winchester rifle and carbine calibres, such as the .38/40 in 1886 and the .32/20 in 1887. E. C. Woodley, who first went to cowboying in 1888 and was a deputy sheriff in the nineties, commented that the .32/20 became very popular with peace officers in the 1890's.

Before 1882, Colts were usually furnished with one piece walnut grips, but after 1882 the grips were made in two pieces of molded black hard rubber. Shy Ousterhout remarked that grips were sometimes marked with cattle brands, initials, or set with steel tacks. Most cowboys bought Colts with barrels shorter than the Army length, usually from four and three quarters to seven inches. Extra long barrels could be ordered, at extra cost, and these were very rare. Medium barrel lengths were most favored by cowboys, usually about five inches.

Since the cowboy's revolver was intended for hard and long use, he very seldom sported a fancy weapon — engraved or specially plated. Nearly all revolvers were finished in plain metallic blue. Once in a while, a revolver with special pearl, bone, or ivory grips was seen among the cowboys, but not very often. Teddy

Blue Abbott recalled one instance where the owner of a large outfit rewarded his favorite wagon boss with a gift of a "forty-five dollar single action . . . with an ivory handle, and an N bar set in gold in it".

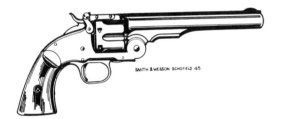

SMITH & WESSON SCHOFIELD 45

One frequent misconception about cowboy armament is the romantic tradition of the two-gun man; seen striding across the stage of fiction and movie screens with two revolvers belted on his hips — supposedly bringing both into play at once, with unerring accuracy. The facts were, that the two-gun cowboy was a rarity — or a very green newcomer to the range country. Some professional gunmen did carry two guns, but as Ben Bird observed, "the kind of fellows that did carry two would carry one in the scabbard and hide-out gun down under their arms. If he had two guns, he sure didn't let people see the second one". The origin of the two-gun myth goes back about thirty years before 1881, to the era of slow loading percussion cap and ball revolvers. In the percussion days, some men did wear two guns, but not to shoot them simultaneously. Because they took so much longer to load than the cartridge revolvers of the middle 1870's through 1890's, two percussion guns were worn to give the wearer twelve instead of only six shots at his command before having to reload. Percussion revolvers became obsolete after the early 1870's, when cartridge arms rapidly replaced them. Jake Tomamichel recalled seeing only one percussion revolver carried in the 1880's, and that was by a thirteen-year-old boy. Many percussion Colts and Remingtons were converted to use metallic cartridges in the early 1870's though, and some were likely carried by cowboys.

While Colt single actions were the most popular and predominant cowboy weapons, other makes were also in use to a limited degree by cowpunchers of the 1880's. The idea of a double action, self-cocking revolver was not new, but until Colt brought out its Lightning model revolvers in 1877, it had not been adapted to modern American hand guns. The Colt Lightning is similar in appearance to the single action, in frame, barrel, cylinder, and ejector; but the trigger guard is different and the grips were the smaller "bird-head" type instead of the square butt variety used in the single action. Lightning grips are round at the bottom, and smaller than those on the 1872 single action. The internal mechanism permits this revolver to be cocked and fired either single or double action; a single squeeze of the trigger revolved the cylinder into firing position, brought the hammer back, and released the hammer to strike the cartridge primer. The Lightning was widely marketed by Colt, but never became very popular on the open range. According to Harry Schlosher and Harvey Robinson, the Lightning's internal mechanism was too delicate and likely to get out of adjustment. It came in two styles with a medium barrel length and ejector along the right side of the barrel, or in a short barrel length without the ejector. This particular Colt came in two calibres, .38 and .41. A few of these Lightnings were used by cowboys. Writing in 1950, one old cowboy recalled that he had "packed a double action, .41 Colt in the holster of my saddle". One disadvantage of the Lightning was that its ammunition did not interchange with any of the Winchester rifles or carbines.

What had been said of the Colt Lightning was also true to some extent of the Smith & Wesson revolvers. These arms "broke" at the top of the frame to load, and looseness often resulted from hard usage and wear on the hinge. Very few Smith & Wessons were used by cowboys, and were more likely carried by surveyors and peace officers. One of the chief features of the Smith & Wesson was the automatic ejection of empty shells when the revolver was opened for loading. This was effected by a collar set into the center of the cylinder at the rear that popped the empty cases out. If one opened a S&W to reload a couple of fired chambers, he had to be careful not to eject his remaining loaded shells as well. Smiths that did see some use on the open range were the 1869 "American" model and the Schofield that came out a few years later. The Army used a few Schofields, in two out of ten cavalry regiments, but did not adopt them for general issue as was the case with the 1872 model Colt single action, which was adopted for cavalry and artil-

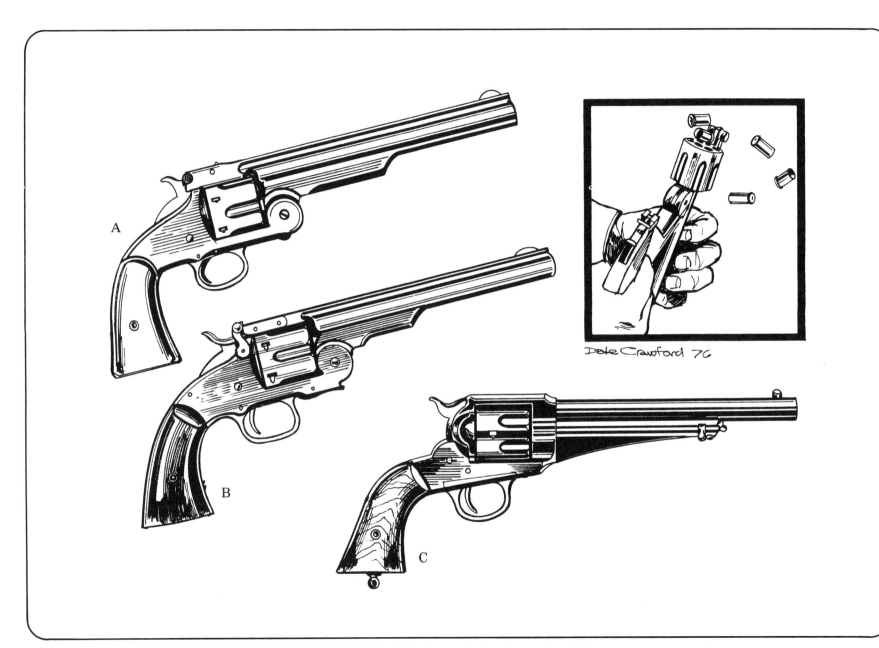

A

B

C

Dale Crawford 76

(A) Smith & Wesson "American", model 1869, .44 calibre.

(B) Smith & Wesson "Schofield", sold to the Army in 1875 — used by some civilians, also made in .44. Both were single-action and "broke" at a hinge on the bottom of the frame, ejecting all the shells at once.

(C) Remington 1875 model, .44 calibre. Indian police on reservations used them in the 1880's and some cowboys had them as well.

lery use in 1873 and remained standard for twenty years.

Though the Remington Arms Company's main emphasis was on the production of rifles and carbines, they did market a single action .44 calibre revolver in 1875 to compete with the Colt. This was a redesign of their percussion army revolver, retaining very similar lines, even to the rib under the barrel which had been the loading lever in the percussion models. Like its predecessor, the cartridge .44 Remington had a solid frame, and unlike the Colt the back-strap and trigger strap, but not the trigger guard, were forged in one piece as part of the frame. The trigger guard was a separate part. Remington grips were usually wood, and two-piece, like the Colts after 1882. Some 1875 Remington revolvers were carried by cowboys, as attested to by the label on one of them displayed in the Range Riders' Museum at Miles City, Montana; "bought in Colorado by a cowboy in 1880". The barrel of this gun has been shortened about an inch; either due to damage to the original muzzle, or perhaps because its owner wanted a shorter barrel. Several hundred .44 Remington model 1875 revolvers were purchased by the Interior Department in the early 1880's, to arm the Indian police on several reservations. All of these were nickle-plated.

Collectors of antique western arms and museum curators will occasionally run across some odd appearing "Peacemakers",

"Frontier Single Actions", and such odd-ball hand guns as "Smith & Weston" which are almost certain to be old Belgian or Spanish-made copies of Colt and Smith & Wesson handguns. Cheap arms have been manufactured in Spain and Belgium, and more recently in Germany and Italy, for a great many years. Such copying really amounted to pirating of arms patented in other countries. Some of these poorly made handguns were sold in this country, or came in from Mexico and South America. It is very doubtful if an arms buyer as discriminating as a cowboy would have purchased such a revolver, as they were badly made and potentially dangerous to the user.

The scabbards, or holsters, used by cowboys to carry revolvers were open topped, and generally of the loop-through type where the body of the holster is looped through a large slotted flap, which forms a wide loop for the cartridge belt to pass through. Most all holsters were of brown or natural colored leather. Some cowboys made their own holsters and cartridge belts from home-tanned "grained" leather. Ben Bird described the graining method of tanning leather; a simple but hard work job: hair and glue was scraped off with a knife, then the inside of the hide was fleshed and evened out the same way; finally a lot of time was spent vigorously rubbing the hide around a pole or tree to soften it. The result was "grained" leather, used not only for holsters and gun belts,

Two types of holsters and belts, and a shoulder holster for in town or winter use. Gunbelts were rarely worn in town.

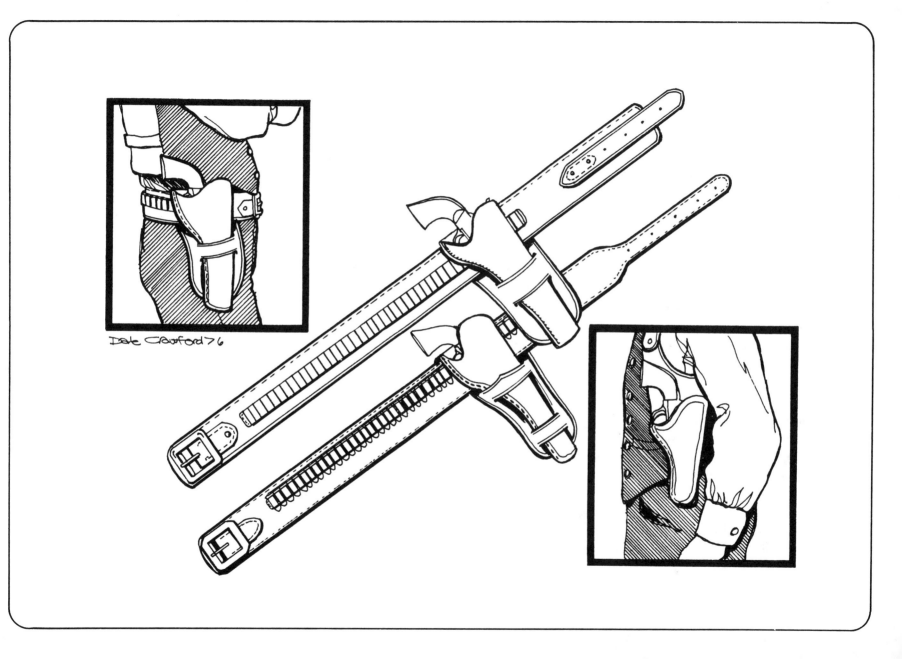

Dale Crawford 76

but for making bridles, ropes, and hobbles as well. This process took a lot of time, but produced tough, pliable first-class leather.

The combined holster and gun belt made of heavy single thickness leather was not used in the eighties, or before 1910. All 1880's holsters were made to slide on to the cartridge belt, and were of leather a little heavier than the belt itself. Though some were home-made, most came from saddle shops. Some had basket stamping designs but most were plain and none were carved, except possibly for the knife-cut decoration of a brand or the owner's initials. This was also true of shoulder holsters. As had already been mentioned, there were other ways of packing a smoke iron rather than in a belt or shoulder holster; especially in town. Sam Hotchkiss commented that cowboys enjoying cultural opportunities in town, and who did not wish to appear uncivilized, occasionally tucked a revolver into a boot top as insurance. The merits of such armament, in social intercourse that most frequently was lubricated with forty-rod pop-skull, are plainly debatable. Many senseless killings did occur; although it was observed that nothing is so conducive to good manners as the society of armed men.

The cartridge belt that carried the revolver holster was usually made of fairly soft calf leather, doubled over and sewn along the top or bottom edge to make a belt three to four inches wide. An opening was sometimes made on the inside of the belt, or its buckle and left unsewn, so that it could also be used as a money belt. Surviving examples are all fastened with medium sized plain white metal or nickled buckles attached to the body of the belt by a narrower separate billet of leather. The tongue was also a separate, narrower billet sewn on the other end of the belt. None of the examples seen were ornamented in any way with tooling, carving or stitching, and gun belt buckles in the 1880's were plain, functional items, not the fancy types later used in rodeos and parades. Cartridge loops usually extended nearly all the way around the belt, holding about forty shells, or, as five old cowmen explained, about as many as came in a box of fifty, allowing for a fill up of the revolver.

Styles of wearing the gun belt varied some; especially so on the northern and southern ranges. Texans seemed to favor wearing the outfit so as to hang the holster a little lower; while northern cowpunchers generally wore theirs' close to the trousers waist band. To insure a smooth and speedy draw, the bottom of the holster was often tied to the thigh with a leather thong, said Ben Bird, but when riding fast, the holster was usually pulled up higher, close to the waist belt.

Very few working cowboys carried hidden "hide-out" guns. None of the 1880's cowboys ever recalled of a cowboy carrying or owning a derringer or other small "stingy gun". Such coat-sleeve and vest pocket artillery were scorned by cowboys as being more the style of tin-horns and con men.

(A) Most of the cartridge belts of this era had an opening in the buckle end of the belt to hold money.

(B) When the billet is run through the slot cut into the belt, and then buckled, it seals off the opening and holds your money inside the belt.

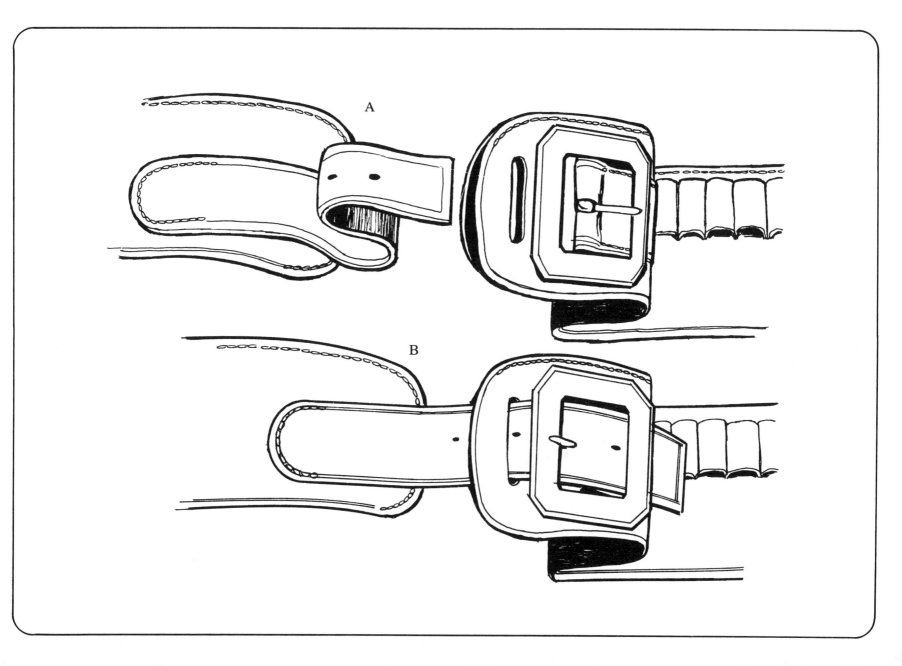

Rifles and Carbines

Once the threat of organized Indian hostilities had passed, very few working cowboys owned or habitually carried a rifle or carbine. After the summer of 1881, when the last sizeable band of hostile Sioux surrendered, cowmen were still wary of reservation runaways and wandering groups of Indians; but the main reason for carrying a rifle or carbine had lessened a great deal in importance. Long arms were not handy to carry for a man who lived on horseback. Working cowboys rarely carried a rifle or carbine, because it could easily get in the way when roping, and because it added just that much more weight to the gear carried on a horse. Ben Bird emphasized that some ranchers wouldn't allow their hands to carry a carbine or rifle for this reason.

Cowboys who did own rifles or carbines usually carried them in plain leather scabbards, or "boots", on either side of the saddle, but generally on the left side, to leave the right side free for the rope, said Shy Ousterhout. Rifles, and the shorter carbines, were sometimes carried when line riding or traveling, never during roundup or other cattle work. On the trail drives, long guns were most likely to go in the bed-roll wagon.

Since there was usually little employment for 1880's cowboys in the winter, some, who had not drifted back south, made a living as market meat hunters — shooting deer, elk, antelope and selling the meat in town. Before the buffalo were killed out on the northern range in 1883, some cowboys were also part-time hide hunters. Harry Schlosher had been a market and buffalo hunter operating out of Miles City, Montana. He turned to cowboying after 1883, but kept his .45/90 calibre "Old Reliable" model 1874 Sharps rifle during his cowboy years in the eighties. This particular Sharps was a sixteen pound rifle, usually fired from a rest, by using either a wiping rod or two crossed sticks. Though it was chambered for the commercial .45/90 cartridge — a .45 lead bullet of about five hundred grains backed by a charge of ninety grains of black powder in a brass shell — it would also take the universally obtainable .45/70 Government ammunition. Jake Tomamichel had also owned a Sharps rifle in the eighties. Jake explained that he had bought his from a buffalo hunter for only ten dollars in 1885. The gun had cost about $125.00 when new, but the hunter was suffering from a hard case of the shorts — and the buffalo were gone. This

Dale Crawford 12-75

Rifles
Hide and meat hunters, which some cowboys were at times, used a cross-sticks dead-rest for accuracy.
Top to bottom:
 Sharps rifle, .45-90 calibre, Model 1874 — a reach-out and knock-down weapon — single shot and deadly.
 Remington, .44-77 calibre, contemporary with Sharps and about as popular and effective.
 Springfield, U.S. Infantry rifle, .45-70 calibre, Model 1884. Gov't ammunition could be used in the .45-90, and a lot was.

was also an "Old Reliable" Sharps, but manufactured in .45/70 calibre.

Other models of Sharps were also in use in the 1880's. Thousands had been converted from percussion to metallic cartridges in the years after the Civil War. Most of these were short carbines, but there were also some of the longer infantry model rifles. Many converted Sharps were altered to take the .50 calibre Government ammunition used in Army weapons from 1866 to 1874, but some were re-barreled to use the more modern .45/70 cartridge. All were single shot. Shy Ousterhout used one of these converted carbines for hunting in winter. During an Indian scare in Dakota Territory in 1880, a number of ranch hands were armed with these Sharps carbine saddle guns. Sharps arms were noted for on-the-mark long range accuracy, and most commercial models had double set triggers; the rear trigger "set" the forward one; which would fire the gun with just the lightest touch of the trigger finger, so as not to disturb the shooter's aim. Aside from the calibres mentioned, Sharps were also made in .44/77, a variety of .40 and .45 calibre heavy powder charge ammunition, up to and including the .50/100, which was very rare.

Civilians could occasionally buy condemned, or new, .45/70 Springfield single-shot Army rifles and carbines. A few of these were used by cowmen, as recalled by Harry Schlosher. Most of

A

B

C

D

Winchesters

(A) Henry .44 rim-fire rifle, early 1860's.
(B) Model 1866, carbine — an improvement on the Henry, mainly by loading at the side of the frame — but using the same modest cartridges in the tube magazine under the barrel. Both had brass frames.
(C) Model 1873 carbine, iron frame — first in .44 Winchester Center Fire or .44-40 calibre — the same as many Colts — better than the .44 Henry, but not much.
(D) Model 1876 rifle — same action design as the 1873, but much heavier to take the .45-70 Gov't and other powerful ammunition.

these were the models of 1873 and 1884 Springfields, which, due to the long firing pin, were generally referred to in the 1880's as "needle-guns". A lot of earlier .50/70 Springfields, made between 1866 and 1874, were traded to Indians after they were declared obsolete and condemned by the Army after 1874.

By all odds, the lever-action repeating Winchesters were the most popular long arms with the cowboys who did own and use rifles or carbines in the 1880's. The first Winchester was the model 1866, an improvement on the earlier Henry that saw limited use during the Civil War. Like the Henry, they were made for .44 copper-cased, rim-fire ammunition that could not be reloaded. The first Winchesters had brass frames, butt plates, and forestock caps. Ben Bird observed that there were still a few Henry and 1866 Winchesters in use in the eighties, although improved models had been on the market for many years.

In 1873, Winchester brought out a much improved carbine and rifle taking a more powerful, accurate, and center-fire reloadable cartridge; the .44/40. Shy Ousterhout agreed with Ben Bird and all the other old cowmen in emphasizing that the .44/40, model 1873 Winchester carbine was by far the most favored long arm of 1880's cattlemen. This carbine had an iron frame and all iron fittings, except for the cartridge carrier just forward of the trigger-guard, which was made of brass. Colt single-action revolvers were also chambered for the .44/40 shell. "Model 1873" is found stamped on the action tang of these weapons, just behind the hammer. Like the Colts, the 1873 Winchester was later made in .38/40 and .32/20 in the eighties as well as the .44/40. The calibre of a rifle or carbine will usually be found stamped on the under side of the brass cartridge carrier and on top of the barrel as ".44 W.C.F.", which would indicate .44/40 Winchester Center Fire.

In 1876, Winchester brought out a heavier "Centennial" version of the model 1873. This was a much larger weapon, over-all, but designed to take purely rifle cartridges, such as the .45/70 Government, the .45/60, and the .45/75. These were intended for serious business, big game hunting and long range shooting. The 1876 model Winchesters were heavy and too long and unwieldy for use on horseback, and very few of them were used by working cowboys. Market and hide hunters made the widest use of the model 1876 Winchester in the eighties. The Royal Canadian North-west Mounted Police were equipped with a special model of the 1876 Winchester in .45/75 calibre during the 1880's, and used them in the short-lived half-breed and Indian rebellion led by Louis Riel in 1885.

In the middle 1880's, Winchester brought out another type of heavy calibre rifle and carbine as the model 1886. This is a much stouter action. Quite a few of them are still seen in the northern range country. Harvey Robinson and Harry Schlosher each recalled using an 1886 model Winchester, in .40/82 calibre, just before 1890.

All the heavy calibre ammunition for Sharps, Remingtons, and Winchesters, in fact all metallic cartridges, were quite expensive in the 1880's. Because of the cost factor, cowboys, like many other arms users, commonly reloaded their empty cartridge shells. Rim-fire cartridges could not be reloaded, which was one reason for their pretty well going out of use after 1880 for other than .22 calibre and other low pressure ammunition. Winchester, Marlin, and other firms sold reloading tools and bullet moulds for refilling all types of center-fire ammunition. A considerable saving could be made by casting lead bullets and reloading saved shells with the simple "nutcracker" tong tools; an occupation often left for long winter evenings and other slack times.

While repeating lever action "saddle guns" were the most popular cowboy long arms of the eighties, some single shot weapons, other than the Sharps, were sometimes carried by traveling or line riding cowboys. Remington developed a simple yet very strong single shot breech-loading action toward the end of the Civil War. This rolling block action, and the Whitney which is very like it, was made in rifle and carbine lengths for the commercial market. Harry Schlosher remarked that these were occasionally seen among cattlemen; usually in .45/70, .44 rimfire, or .44/40 calibres.

Most of the firearms-related violence among cowboys was of the random type, often in a range country saloon or in town, when carbines and rifles were not present but revolvers were. There were exceptions though, when long guns figured in the settlement of personal differences.

Jake Tomamichel was present at such a fatal shooting incident at an eastern Montana ranch headquarters in the late 1880's. There had been a poker game in the bunkhouse, and an argument flared up between an older married man and the outfit's black cook. "That cook was mean clear through", said Jake, "and he hadn't a friend in the outfit. One of the hands, a Texan we all thought was more a gunman than a cowman, took up the fight for the married fella when the cook went to the cook-shack to get his rifle. As the cook came back busting through the door, the Texan shot him five times". Jake emphasized the cook's unpopularity, explaining that no inquest was held or mention made of the shooting, and the cook was buried the same night without a tear shed. The fact that the cook was black may have had something to do with the attitude taken toward his killing; although by and large, 1880's cowboys had less racial prejudice than most men of their time. There were more than a few black cowboys in the eighties, a number of part-blood Indian cowpunchers, and quite a few Mexican vaqueros. If a man was a good hand, that really was what mattered the most on the open range of the 1880's.

On the whole, rifles and carbines saw more use among cowboys in the eighties on the northern ranges than in the south. Maybe because there was more big game to hunt, maybe because the Indian threat lasted longer there. In any case, as Ben Bird observed since most cowboys "could hunt with a pistol", the carrying of long arms was never common among open range cattlemen.

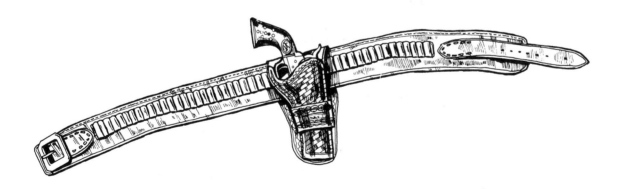

Knives

All outdoorsmen know the many uses to which a good knife can be put, and open range cowboys almost always had a sturdy knife or two with them at all times. The most popular knife was a large, rugged pocket or clasp knife; very often a "Barlow". According to E. C. Woodley, the IXL knives were very popular. Very few 1880's cowboys favored wearing a belt or hunting knife. Of those who did, a knife with about a five inch blade was most popular. Most belt knives were quite plain, and if one were seen with some silver inlay on the handle or otherwise ornamented, it was almost certain to have come from Mexico, commented Ben Bird.

A few cowboys of the eighties carried a knife for use as a weapon rather than a tool, but this was rare. Shy Ousterhout recalled that a former Texas Ranger working in the Little Missouri country always wore a long double-edged pointed dirk. Harry

I*XL (I Excel) brand knives were tops — made in Sheffield, England by George Wostenholm. Both two-bladed and the single-bladed "barlow" types were very popular. Cowboys bet money and knives in mumbletypeg matches as a pastime.

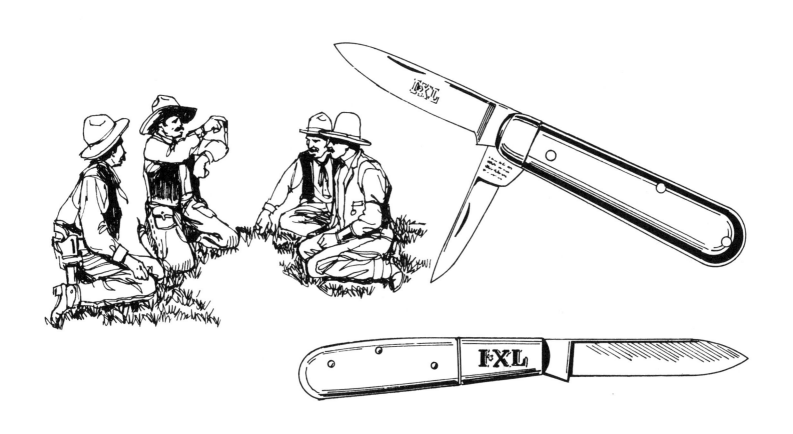

Schlosher said that there were a few hard cases and would-be badmen who carried a short sheath knife in a scabbard in their pocket, or perhaps tied the sheath inside the top of a boot leg. Ben Bird knew one man who had his knife sheath rivetted to his boot leg. These knives were not the large Bowie type of earlier frontier fame.

Knife throwing and gambling on skill at knife tricks and games were very popular cowboy recreation pastimes, in much the same way that pistol shooting was popular. Mumbletypeg was a great favorite.

Because they were working with cattle, and also did quite a bit of hunting, many cowboys had skinning knives in their kits. Sam Hotchkiss and Ben Bird explained that these were the common curved blade skinning knife that is still in use. When cattle were "winter killed", or died on the range, cowmen generally skinned the carcass for the hide, so that the animal was not a total loss. Hides were about all that was saved from the thousands and thousands of cattle that died in the terrible winter of 1886-87, when many cattlemen were wiped out.

Ropes

A throw rope was almost as important to a cowboy as his horse, and in the open range years, roping was developed to its high point as a working cowboy skill. The cowpuncher of the 1880's took great pains with and good care of his rope. It was his main tool in working cattle. It was never called a "lasso", said Ben Bird, and was most often termed a "catch rope or throw rope", according to Jake Tomamichel and Harry Schlosher. On the plains, ropes were usually forty to fifty feet long, to throw a small loop, made of about seven sixteenth of an inch stock. Far western cowboys generally used longer ropes and bigger loops, but the men who came up from Texas used a small loop, because they were used to roping in brush country. Some ropes were as short as thirty feet, and others over fifty, but most fell somewhere between.

Ropes were made with a variety of materials in the eighties, but about two thirds of the open range plains cowmen favored a rawhide rope. A good many rawhide ropes were braided by the men who used them, using either three or four strands of suppled rawhide in much the same way as sailors braid rope. Saddler shops of the eighties carried these ropes in stock as well, usually the product of winter slack time work by cowboys.

Other ropes were made of "seagrass", Mexican maguey fibre, sisal and a very few of braided horsehair. Harry Schlosher explained that grass and fibre ropes were rough and prickly when new, and were sometimes laid on a pile of paper, then the paper was lit, to burn off loose fibres. Hemp ropes were not used in the 1880's.

Since the slip loop is the most important part of the rope, great care and skill was employed in fashioning the slip honda, or "hondu". Usually, the slip was only carefully tied into the end of a rope, as small as possible to offer the least resistance to wind and the lightest weight at the rope's working end. Metal "hondus" were sometimes braided into the end of a rope, to provide the easiest slippage for the line. Not too many cowboys used these metal "hondus" though. Ben Bird and Harvey Robinson explained that one could easily knock out a horse's eye with one when roping, and they were otherwise dangerous when swung at the business end of a throw rope. Harry Schlosher recalled that there was a fad among some cowpunchers in the eighties for these special

To supple-up a rawhide rope it was run through two holes in a heavy plank, then pulled back and forth — a lot of work in a rawhide rope, but they were the best.

The slip or "hondu" had to be as small as possible, yet allow for slippage and still be strong enough to hold.

Dale Crawford 76

brass and iron "hondus", and there were some who carved them out of deer and mountain sheep horns.

Two general styles of roping had become well fixed by the 1880's as to the best way to use a rope. Aside from the large vs. small loop, there was a major difference of opinion as to how the rope should best be anchored to the saddle horn. Oregon and Pacific coast cowboys were generally called "dally welters", because they did not tie the end of the rope to the saddle horn, but only took a couple of turns, or "dallies", with the end of the rope around the horn; a cowboy rendering of the Spanish "dar la vuelta". This was a tricky and dangerous business, and could easily cost a man a thumb or some of his fingers if they got tangled between the rope and the horn. Great plains cowmen usually tied the rope's end securely to the horn, as a firm hold when the rope was on a fractious cow or horse. The rope was usually carried on the right side, for ready use, either tied to the saddle or slung over the horn.

Trick and fancy roping was very popular, and some men spent much of their leisure time practising and perfecting their skills with a well greased rawhide rope. Rope tricks early became features of wild west shows, and later carried over into vaudeville. Will Rogers got his show business start as a rope artist, twirling loops for Ziegfield audiences.

Quirts

Nearly every cowpuncher used a riding quirt in the 1880's. Carried by a thong looped around his wrist, it was as much a part of his riding gear as were his spurs. Every outfit's "cavy", or horse remuda had a few bad actors, and the rawhide quirt was strong medicine for such half-broken saddle broncos. The body, or handle was from six to twelve inches long, sometimes filled with lead small shot to give it weight, though often of iron or wood around which the rawhide was carefully and often very artistically braided. A limber section of braided rawhide extended for another six to ten inches, and the quirt was topped off with a popper of two leather or rawhide thongs of about the same length. Aside from riding, a loaded handle quirt was a very effective weapon in rough and tumble fighting or a saloon brawl. The weighted handle was a useful black-jack, and a hefty punch from a fist wrapped around the same was bad medicine for whoever it connected with.

Like rawhide ropes and other braided horse gear, quirts were very commonly made by the men who used them. Some cowboys braided quirts as a pastime, and sold them to other cowboys or to saddle shops in town. Much of this work was very skillfully done, using fancy knots and braiding. Quirts seemed to go out of style somewhat after 1900, but were used all over the open range before then.

Gentling a spooky horse in the morning was a lot easier with a good heavy quirt.

Dale Crawford 76

Canteens and Waterbags

Though range riding in what was usually a very dry country, very few cowboys carried canteens or waterbags. Though their lack was often keenly felt, they were just too much extra to pack on a cow pony. On roundups and on trail drives, water was carried in a barrel on the cook and bedroll wagon. As Ben Bird put it, when away from the wagon, a cowboy "lay down and drank like a cow when water was found". Canteens were generally considered unnecessary by men who slaked their thirst by getting a "drink out of a cow-track filled with rainwater", according to Harry Schlosher.

Once in a while, Shy Ousterhout recalled, a cowboy would be seen travelling across country with a round canteen marked "US" tied to his saddle; which had been traded from a soldier, but this was uncommon.

A few cowboys had Army canteens, mostly in the desert Southwest. A quart of warm pond water could taste like a mountain spring to a dried out rider.

Bedrolls

The open range cowpuncher was often away from the ranch bunkhouse and he needed easily portable sleeping gear when trailing herds, riding distant parts of his range, and on roundups. Specially designed outdoor sleeping bags had not yet been developed, so the 1880's cowboy made his own. The open range cowboy's bedroll was composed of a medium weight canvas tarpaulin, with enough quilts and/or blankets inside it to keep him moderately dry and warm. All such bedrolls were "built in a tarp", explained Ben Bird and Sam Hotchkiss, about eighteen feet long and six feet wide, that was doubled over from the bottom up and tucked under the sleeper on each side. Some tarps were waterproofed with paint, most were not. Shy Ousterhout recalled that a few tarps were seen with a series of rings and snaps sewn on the sides, to help keep the bedroll together. This may have been the origin of the modern sleeping bag.

Heavy canvas over "soogan" quilts and blankets was the cowboy's bedroll — "warbag", extra clothes, and anything else he wasn't wearing or using were rolled up in it in the daytime or in camp.

Inside the tarp, the cowboy layered from two to four "soogans", or light cotton quilts, or, as Harry Schlosher and Jake Tomamichel explained, "a combination of soogans and blankets". The origin of the word "soogan" has been lost, though the word is still current among some cattlemen in the West.

Harry Schlosher commented that the hard twist virgin wool gray army blankets of the times were much favored by cowboys. Like other army gear, blankets could frequently be traded from soldiers; usually at the rate of a quart of booze per blanket, said Shy Ousterhout. But most 1880's bedrolls were made up of "soogans" instead of blankets.

Other than army blankets, a few other types were especially favored by cowboys. The heavy "California" blankets, costing $18.00 each, were highly prized by cowpunchers who could afford them, observed Harry Schlosher, since they were almost twice as heavy as army blankets. A few open range riders also used Mexican or Navajo blankets, but only a very few.

The cheapest type of bedroll blanket was a thin article known as a "henskin". These were cheap indeed, costing only about a dollar six bits each, and woven with about eight threads of cotton to one of wool. They wore out quickly, but a good many cowboys used them as a sheet in the bedroll.

Open range custom demanded the utmost in hospitality to

strangers, and if a stranded stranger happened into camp lacking a bedroll, cowboys were expected to share some blankets with him. Jake Tomamichel remarked that this was sometimes grudging hospitality. Not a few range riders hosted lice, and cowpunchers were understandably reluctant to offer this ultimate in hospitality. The only way to really delouse blankets in such a case was to spread them on an active ant hill, for the ants to eat the unwelcome greybacks.

Cowboys did not carry a pillow for the bedroll, but usually wadded up a coat or extra clothes, or bunched up their warbag for a pillow. In traveling and on roundups, the bedrolls were generally carried in the cook wagon or an extra bed wagon. When the cowboy was traveling on his own, or representing his outfit at a distant roundup, he usually carried his bedroll and other gear on a pack horse.

Warbags

This article of 1880's cowboy gear, whose name was plainly borrowed from the Indians, served as his valise and catch-all for a variety of small items and extra clothes he carried with him away from the bunk house. Like the Indian's warbag, that of the cowboy was meant for stowage of essential articles of dress and equipment not worn by the cowpuncher all the time or carried on his horse. The universal warbag of the eighties was a seamless canvas two-bushel grain sack. Sometimes the open end was sewn shut and a slit made in the middle, explained Sam Hotchkiss, through which extra clothes and other items carried in the sack could be placed and spread inside it. Other warbags, said Ben Bird, were closed by merely tieing a thong around the mouth of the sack, or perhaps by punching holes along the open edge and lacing a string or thong through the holes.

For identification purposes, some cowboys marked their

A traveling cowboy's extra clothes and small possessions were stowed in the "warbag".

D.R. ⅄

names, initials, or brands on their warbags. It was commonly carried rolled up in the bedroll and used as a pillow at night. Harry Schlosher said that the contents of a man's warbag was "something like two suits of underwear, a spare shirt, some socks, and a little loose personal stuff". Open range cowboys often traveled far, and they almost always traveled light.

Cowboy Gear

Saddles and Horse Gear

Because the open range cattle industry expanded north from the Texas-Mexico border country, much of the dress and equipment showed definite Mexican influences in the 1880's. This was especially true of the stock saddles ridden by the cowboys of the eighties. Evolving from Mexican saddles, which in turn had been derived from earlier Spanish war saddles, the cowboy saddle of the 1880's had a very high cantle and was always full skirted. Ben Bird observed that some of the Texas saddles ridden north in the trail drives of the 1880's actually had been made in old Mexico, where saddle-making was a high art. Only a very few such saddles were showy and highly ornamented though, as such horse gear was rare among cowpunchers in the eighties. A few fashion plate kind of punchers, the "shadow watcher" sort, actually rode a "ten dollar horse and forty dollar saddle" in the words of "The Old Chisholm Trail" verse. What decoration there was usually amounted to stamped flower designs or basket weave on the leather, especially the skirting — not in carving, coloring, and ornamenting with silver.

Most of the stock saddles made since 1900 are of the swell-fork types, where the front fork or pommel of the saddle tree is swelled out from either side of the fork. As Shy Ousterhout and Harvey Robinson commented, there were no swell-fork saddles in the early days, and all cowboy saddles were of the "straight A", or slick fork variety. The iron or wooden horn top was flat, and often left uncovered as well — a stout peg to anchor your throw rope with a tie down or couple of dallies when a contrary-minded horse or cow was on the other end.

In the range country east of the Rockies in the eighties, most saddles were of the double rigged or "rim-fire" type. These had two cinches instead of one. The name "rim-fire" came from the forked firing pin of the Henry and 1866 model Winchesters leaving a striker dent on each side of the rim of the .44 calibre rim-fire cartridge case — a term generally applied to a double rigged saddle. Single rig saddles that came from the Pacific slope ranges were termed "center-fire", due to the single cinch ring on the saddle rigging. Some of these were seen on the open range east of the Rockies, but not very many.

A third type of saddle rigging, that developed from "center-fire" types, was the Montana or three-quarter rigged saddle that Ben Bird and Harry Schlosher said were sometimes seen in the northern range country. In the Montana rig, the saddle was fitted with two rings leading to the cinch ring.

Because the cowboy's saddle was first and foremost a functional article, the double rigged saddle, where the saddle is most firmly anchored to the horse, was the most popular for hard and fast roping. With a single cinch, explained Harry Schlosher, the saddle could be turned almost sideways with a tough old cow or wild horse on the end of your rope. On the great plains ranges, the cowboy usually tied his rope securely to the saddle horn when working cattle.

Several types of saddles were popular in the 1880's. A saddle with either a Cheyenne (double rigged) or a Visalia (single rigged) tree could be bought for about thirty-five to forty dollars in 1887. Ben Bird observed that Collins-made saddles were quite popular in the eighties. It too was a double rigged saddle. These 1880's saddles were built by glueing the wooden parts of the tree together and covering with damp rawhide, allowing the rawhide to shrink iron hard, and finally covering the whole with oak tanned leather.

The Moran Brothers, of Miles City, Montana Territory, were among the earliest purveyors of saddles in the Montana-Dakota range country recalled Sam Hotchkiss, Harry Schlosher, and Ben

Saddles and Gear
(A) F. H. Meanea saddle, of Cheyenne, Wyoming Territory. The kind the cowboys loved. Double rigged for one man roping.
(B) Mother Hubbard Saddle.
(C) Taps, or tapaderos used mostly in the Southwest to protect feet from brush.
(D) Full-double rigging, or rim fire. It got its name from the Henry cartridge. When fired, the double firing pin left a mark on each side of the rim of the casing.
(E) ¾ double-rigging.
(F) Center fire rigging.

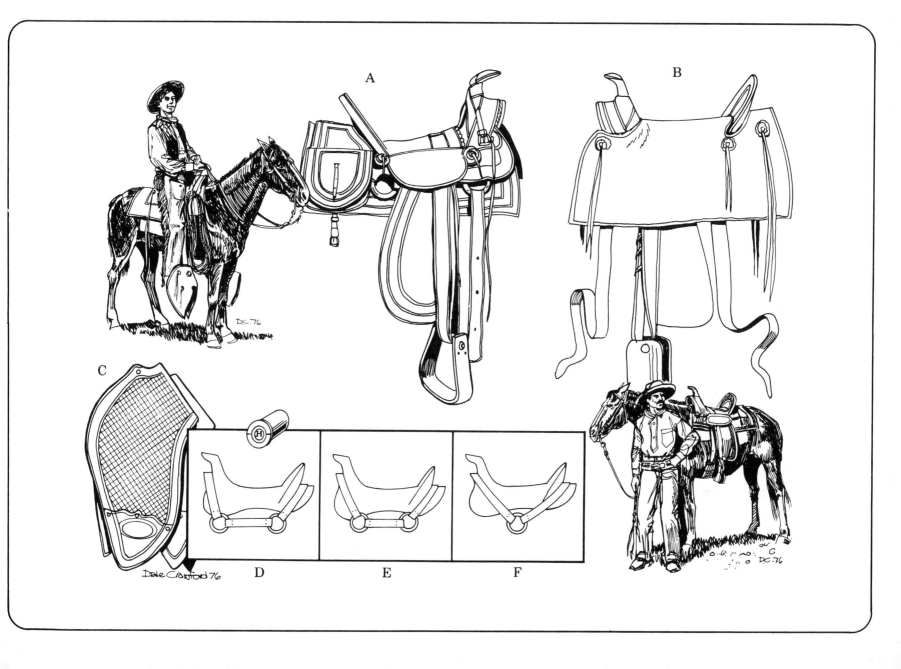

A

B

C

D　　　　　E　　　　　F

DC.76

Dale Crawford 76

DC.76

Bird. Some Moran saddles were made to order; others were made up in advance, as individual likes and variations in rigging could be fitted to any saddle. A little later, the Rattan Saddlery, in Dickinson, Dakota Territory, also supplied saddles and other items of horse gear to the open range cattlemen.

Two good examples of saddles used by cowpunchers on the northern range in the 1880's are in the North Dakota State Historical Society in Bismarck. One was made in Cheyenne, Wyoming Territory, by F. A. Menea, and used on the Connelly brothers' ranch in 1888. This is a double rigged saddle, with a covered iron horn, square russet leather skirts fifteen by twenty-eight inches on a side lined with sheepskin, and rigged with malleable iron ox-bow stirrups. The other stock saddle was used in the same country in the eighties, but had been made in Mexico in 1879 and brought to Dakota Territory in 1884. It is also covered with russet leather, but has full flower stamped designs, square fifteen by twenty-eight inch skirts, leather tie strings and conchos, and the more common wooden ox-bow stirrups.

One style of saddle used by some cowboys as late as the 1880's that is no longer seen, nor has been for many years remarked Shy Ousterhout, was the covered or "macheer" saddle. The "macheer" saddle, explained Harry Schlosher, was an ordinary slick fork stock saddle with a "mochilla" or over-all covering of thin leather

— to reduce friction at all possible points where the rider sat the saddle. Ousterhout and Schlosher added that most saddles in the eighties had wooden ox-bow stirrups, though some iron ones were seen. Cowboys of those times generally rode with a long stirrup leather, said Jake Tonamichel.

Stirrup hoods, called "tapaderos", or "taps", were common in the southwestern range country. Many cowboys brought this style north with them to the northern ranges, where they were often discarded, according to Harvey Robinson and Sam Hotchkiss. "Taps" were originally meant to protect the rider's feet in dense brush country. Some were of the elongated "eagle bill" or "hog snout" types, and very long — perhaps up to twenty-eight inches, tapering to a point. Harry Schlosher commented that such extra long "taps" sometimes had lead weights at the tips, so that a rider could kick forward and whip his horse's head up out of the brush. Fancy parade saddles are often rigged with "taps", which are frequently much decorated.

The most popular cinch in the 1880's was the fishcord cinch, made of many strands of tough, hard twisted cord of about one third inch diameter strung by the cowboys themselves. Some made their cinches from strands of soft latigo leather run through the cinch rings. Hair cinches were also quite popular, and sometimes a diamond design was worked into them.

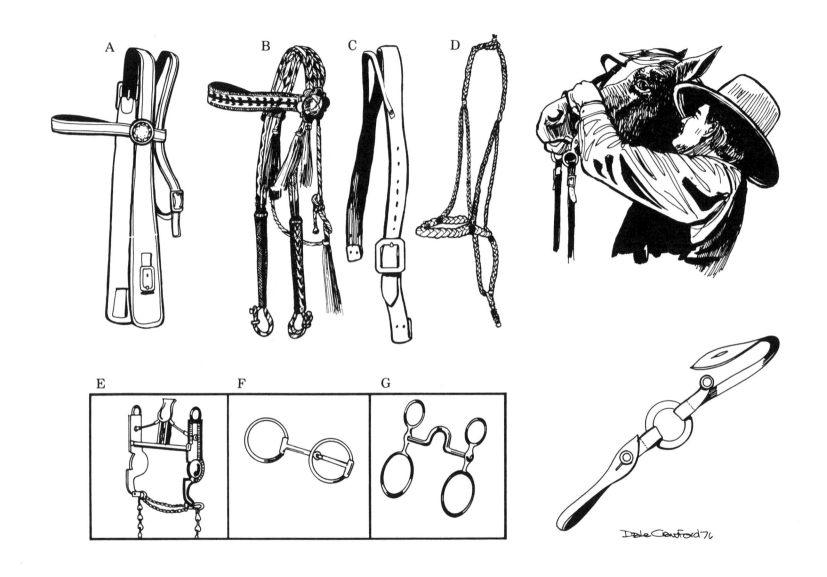

A

B

C

D

E

F

G

Dale Crawford 76

Head Stalls
Four basic kinds:
(A) Common headstall, with brow band to help keep it in place.
(B) Woven horse hair bridle.
(C) Homemade bridle out of a cowboy's belt. The splits went over the horse's ears.
(D) The hackamore — needed no bit — a properly trained horse would respond to the slightest touch of the reins.

Bits
(E) The spade — a cruel bit.
(F) Snaffle bit.
(G) The curb bit — this and the snaffle were used most because they were easy on the horse.
(H) Rawhide horse hobbles.

The three most common and popular saddle blankets used by cowpunchers of the eighties were the grey army blanket, hand woven Mexican and Navajo blankets, and pads and blankets made of horsehair. Sam Hotchkiss and Harry Schlosher said that army blankets were very good, and could generally be traded from soldiers for booze.

Many of the bridles, halters and "theodores" used in the 1880's were made by the cowboys themselves. In isolated areas it was a common thing for a fellow to buy only the iron bit and fit it with straps from scrap leather or hair rope, according to Ben Bird and Shy Ousterhout. Some even made their own bits, added Harry Schlosher, or they were hammered out by local blacksmiths. Home-made bridles naturally showed a good deal of personal preference and individuality, but hardly any used in the eighties were decorated with silver, brass, or nickle-plated tacks. Cowboys who ran to fancy bridles were more likely to satisfy the itch by making or buying a bridle rigged with bands, reins and trailers made of carefully knotted horsehair — sometimes with a diamond braid design. Horsehair bridles often showed geometric patterns in black and white hair, and sometimes with reddish hair for color. Braiding horsehair took a lot of time, considerable skill and plenty of patience, and there never were a great many cowboys who took the pains to make horsehair bridles.

Several kinds and variations of bits were used in the 1880's. Mexican influence was plain in the Spanish spade bits brought north from Texas by the trail drivers, and there were several variations of this cruel bit. Not many remained in use on the northern ranges, as they were very hard on the horse's mouth, and lots of outfits would not allow their hands to use them on company horses. Shy Ousterhout recalled that his father's store had stocked lots of snaffle, ring-bits because lots of the northern cowpunchers favored these. The snaffle was not nearly so hard on a horse, and you could leave the bit in place most of the time, since the horse could drink and graze with the bit in his mouth. Most cowboy bits were long shanked, to give the rider lots of leverage, and were fitted with a medium to small sized port, the part that presses on the horse's tongue.

Rawhide hobbles were also commonly part of a puncher's horse gear in the 1880's, said Ben Bird and Sam Hotchkiss. The hobble shackles, the two loops fitting around the forelegs, were about two to three inches wide, connected by a strap about eighteen inches long. When not in use, hobbles were generally carried slung across the horse's neck, just in front of the saddle. Properly hobbled, a horse could be left to graze at night, or when one were dismounted for any length of time, without his being able to wander too far away from his rider. Cow ponies were com-

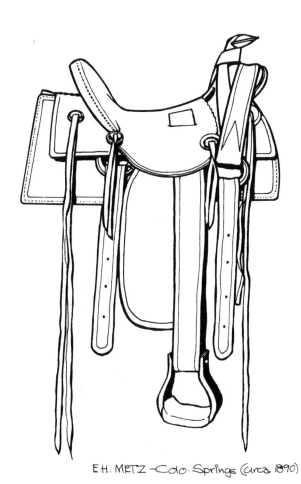

monly trained to stand when the reins were thrown over the head and lying on the ground.

Some cowboys also carried iron picket pins, to stake the horse out on a soft rope at night, but these were not common in the eighties. Many men simply tied their horse to a stout sage or mesquite brush at night.

E.H. METZ – Colo. Springs (Circa 1890)

Branding Irons

Branding stock with red hot irons is inseparably and correctly associated with the open range. Cattle and horses were branded as a way of permanent marking and easy identification. Brand reading was a high art, and open range cowboys prided themselves on their ability to quick-read brands. The usual branding tool was a stamp iron. The wrought iron brand design was hammered out and forged together by a blacksmith, then it was in turn forge-welded to a long iron rod handle. The red hot stamp iron brand was a permanent and indelible mark on the cow's hide.

Considerable thought and ingenuity went into the design of a stamp iron brand; the object being to have a brand that was simple, easy to read, and at the same time difficult to efface or alter. A lot of scheming also went into how to alter brands, at least on the part of some free and easy range riders. Most stamp irons were made by local blacksmiths. The brand was then attached to about

Running Irons
Used for "free-handing" brands, touching up poor stamp iron brands, or illegal brand changing.
(A) Horse-shoe shaped to use as a running iron, with green stick handle.
(B) Common running irons.
(C) Cinch ring with green stick handle, for heating and use as a running iron.

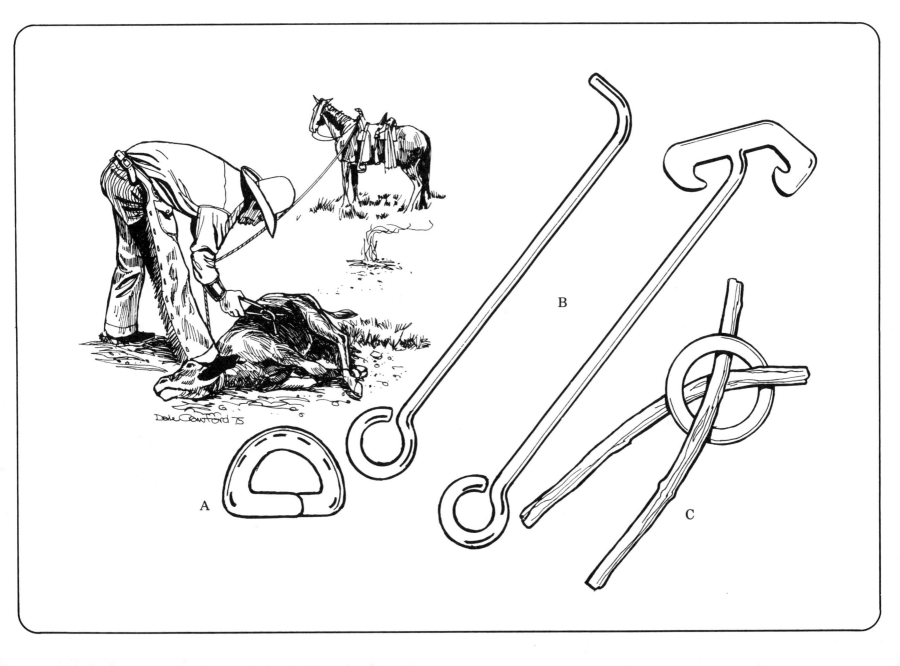

A

B

C

thirty-six to forty-eight inches of half inch iron rod, with a loop handle at the end.

Cowpunchers didn't always carry a stamp iron though, and calves and cows often had to be branded where you found them. For this reason, some fellows carried a special iron cinch ring. The ring could be heated up in a quickly made fire. Then the ring was held by thrusting two sticks through it, and almost any brand could then be made free hand on the hide. This wasn't always considered exactly ethical, as it was a common rustler's practice, and carrying a special cinch ring was sometimes prohibited and otherwise discouraged in polite company.

Another type of branding iron, that was used with a stamp or in place of one, was a handy instrument called a running iron. This was a couple of feet of iron rod, with a small curved projection or bulge at its end. Such irons were used to touch up imperfect brands made by a stamp, or to make a whole brand free-hand. Artistic expression of this type was highly regarded in some circles, but generally frowned upon by the owners of trail herds and big cow outfits. Possession of a running iron by a stranger immediately brought suspicion on him, since running irons were standard equipment for rustlers and illegal brand changers. A cowpuncher wishing to exercise his creativity had much better have done so braiding horsehair, whittling, or leather working than to go in

Brands

Y Cross

J.A.

Hat Brand

Stirrup

Turkey Track

Keystone

Wine Glass

Doorkey

Dan Clay

Lazy Dot — T

Scissors

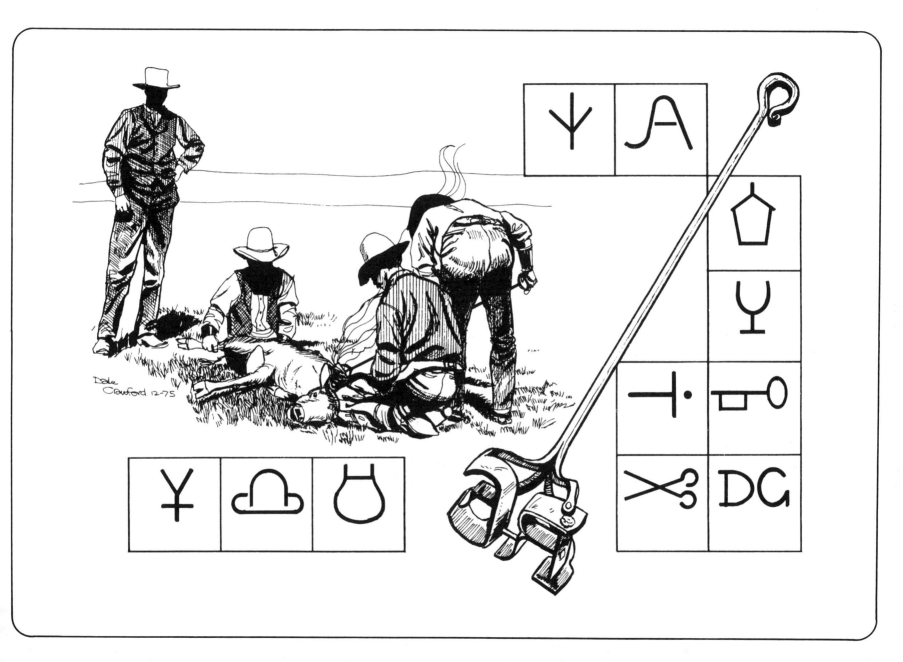

for free hand art with a running iron.

There was lots of other gear used by 1880's open range cowboys other than what has been talked over here, but the articles described were those that were the personal possessions of cowpunchers, or that were used by all of them. Specially braided four-horse whips were used by cooks in driving cook wagons carrying dutch ovens, heavy skillets, and other needed articles and supplies. This material and such articles as chain link mats and drags to fight grass fires were all part of the open range cowboy culture. He also had lanterns, shovels, and other gear — and when the open range days passed he would become very familiar with hay rakes, post-hole diggers, and wire stretchers. But the time before the range was fenced and the water parcelled out to individual owners, when a horsebacker could ride a straight line and not be stopped by a fence, from old Mexico to beyond the British line, have been our interest here. And if things are right at all, the cowmen of the eighties are still riding someplace where the only wire strung is on a telegraph pole, no plough has turned up the heavy buffalo grass sod, and there is lots of room for a fellow to move around in.

Interviews
and Suggested Reading

Some 1880's Cowboys, and Other Information Sources

Most of the information about 1880's cowboy gear came from a series of interviews with men who had been cowboys in the eighties and early nineties. A few of them were known to each other, but the interviews were all individual, and none knew what information the others had given. This way it was possible to compare a variety of replies to the same questions; and when all, or nearly all, gave the same but independent answers about some item of dress or gear, the evidence has seemed worth stating as factual. Naturally, in such a wide open subject there will be areas for difference of opinion; however, the information contained in this book has been put to standard tests for historical accuracy, and represents what a sampling of 1880's cowboys recalled of how they dressed, the tools and equipment they used, and the kinds of horse gear they rode. All these old cowmen are gone now, and by way of saying a too late thank you to them for the information they gave, and the privilege of having known them, the brief sketches that follow tell a little about them. Each would make a good biography subject in his own right.

Ben Bird, a spare angular man of medium height and build, was still riding in his nineties, during the mid-1950's. He and his son travelled the rodeo and fair circuit each summer, racing their own string of quarter horses. Affable and interested in relaying his recollections about cowboying in the 1880's, he chose his words very carefully, and if he did not know or recall an answer to a question he quickly said so. Born in 1865, in west Texas, Ben's first away-from-home job was working in the Palo Duro Canyon country as a cowboy in 1881. During the eighties he took part in three long drives to the Montana-Dakota ranges. The last trail herd he helped bring north was in 1895; after which he stayed in the eastern Montana, western North Dakota country for most of his long life as a working cowboy and rancher.

Sam Hotchkiss lived in Miles City in the mid-1950's, having passed on his own modest ranch to his son. He was born in Connecticut, and never quite lost the accent and manner of speech he learned there as a child. A large, out-going man, he recalled coming to the Miles City area with his father at the age of nine in 1880. Sam had always wanted to be a cowboy, and when L. W. Stacey offered him a job trailing cattle from Texas to Miles City in 1888, he grabbed his chance; accompanying Stacey to Texas to buy cattle and bring them north. He did this several times in his youth, and stayed in the cattle business the rest of his life.

George (Shy) Ousterhout's father brought him as a small boy to the Little Missouri River country from Texas in 1882. His father was an ex-Confederate soldier who became a cowman after the Civil War. When the northern great plains country opened up after the Sioux and Cheyenne were corraled, he moved north to the new ranges. Shy didn't become a full fledged cowboy himself until the early 1890's, but recalled much about the cowmen of the eighties. In the mid-1890's, Shy owned a clothing and outfitting store catering to cowboys, and was especially well informed about changes in cowboy outfits. Shy was a slender, loose-hung sort of fellow, very precise in his talk and the essence of friendliness.

Harvey Robinson was born in 1867 in the northern midwest. A slight, leathery sort of man in appearance, he was very soft spoken and candid as an old man. He came to western North Dakota about 1890, when he went to work as a cowboy. His recollections of cowboy life were very unromantic and real, and his recall of detail was quite vivid.

Harry Schlosher of Miles City had come to the area in 1879, when he was fourteen, working for the Diamond R bull train freight outfit out of Bismarck and Mandan, Dakota Territory. Short, heavy set, and plainly of German ancestry, Harry came west from Wisconsin to find an older brother. Linking up with the brother, the two became buffalo hide hunters and meat hunters for the work crews building the Northern Pacific Railroad in 1880. When the buffalo were killed out on the Montana ranges in 1883-84, Harry became a cowboy. Although he moved around a great deal, he kept Miles City as a home base, and never seems to have thrown anything away. In the late 1950's, he still had a basement full of old cowboy gear, bed-rolls, war-bags, and even the cartridge re-loading tools for the Sharp's rifle he'd hunted buffalo with. Harry was a very cheerful, out-and-about old fellow, well known and respected in Miles City, where he was something of a living land-mark. He was interested in many things, once urging me to be sure to see the dinosaur bones displayed in the basement of the high school at Ekalaka, Montana. Explaining why, Harry spread his arms and said, "they got 'em a skull there must be six foot across — with three horns. Jesus, but I'da hated to have had a rope on *that* son of a bitch!" He knew many facets of the old west, from personal experience and participation, and was noted for his veracity and common sense wisdom.

Jake Tomamichel roamed the west, wrangling horses and cowboying, from the time he ran away from home at Ft. Laramie in 1884, at the age of eleven. A lonely, spare old man when I knew him, Jake loved to entertain good company in his little 1880's frame house in Medora, North Dakota. Good company to Jake was someone he could talk to about his years as a bronc fighter and all-around cowman, and who would hum or sing along with him as he fingered old tunes on his mail-order guitar. He never drank or smoked, but had the reputation of being a quiet fellow, and a man not to be fooled around with. Jake's dad was the Hospital Steward at Ft. Laramie in the 1880's, where Jake spent his boyhood. His dad was very ready with the razor strop, and refused to support Jake's musical ambitions by buying him a zither. Jake spent much of his boyhood pestering soldiers at Ft. Laramie, learning his letters and numbers in the post school, and hanging around the outskirts of the "hog ranch" three miles up river from the fort, where he and his friends looked wide-eyed at the painted gals the soldiers came to patronize. Jake always said they were the prettiest touch of color in his young life. He worked the ranges from the British line down to Old Mexico, and always had a quizzical inquiring turn of mind about the lands and peoples he saw. His memories of 1880's cow-punching were harsh and stark, recalling a very hard way of life, but one that he never left. Jake passed through lots of hard times and tough experiences, and as an old man looked back on his life as one of hard work made worthwhile by the adventure that sometimes went with it.

E. C. Woodley spent nearly all his life in the Wyoming-Montana range country. Portly and courteous as an old man, he was a wiry youngster when he went cowboying for the Dana outfit in 1888. Living in Sheridan, Wyoming in the mid-1950's, Woodley was still reticent and careful what he said about the 1892 Johnson County War, as the subject was still a touchy one. He was a deputy sheriff in Johnson County in the nineties, and knew a good deal about personalities and events related to the cattlemens' "invasion" to eliminate suspected small outfit rustlers. Much of his early cowboy experience was on the Crow Reservation, where he knew a number of eminent Crow people such as White-Man-Runs-Him, White Swan, and Curley. His recollections of 1880's cowboying were very matter-of-fact, and he was not inclined to embellish experiences and the accounts of historic events he had gathered over the years.

Reginald Bradley was by all odds the best educated, most cosmopolitan old cowboy I knew. His father was a well-to-do solicitor in a London suburb in the 1880's, and when his draughtsman son wanted to emigrate to the American West, he sent him off with a complete "outfit", including a set of evening clothes and letters of introduction to friends in America. Reg read a lot about the wild west as a youth in England, and when a friend who had already made the journey wrote inviting him to come and work on a ranch in New Mexico, Bradley made plans to leave as soon as possible. In the spring of 1889 he and his pal hired on with a big outfit gathering cattle north of Deming, New Mexico. Come fall, they were cut from the payroll and out of work. After trying to make it in a gold boom north of Albuquerque, Bradley drifted back to Deming, selling off his outfit to get food money as he went. In November he was bumming west from Deming along the railroad. At Bowie Station, Arizona, he was given a square meal by an Army sergeant running a heliograph detail connecting with Ft. Bowie fourteen miles south. Bradley asked about the Army, and considering he was flat broke and had no job prospects, he decided to go to the fort and enlist. He spent the next five years in the 4th U.S. Cavalry, and after discharge went back to cowboying in the Ft. Bidwell country of northern California, spending the rest of his life in ranching and timber work. Reg Bradley never regretted leaving southern Arizona, and at the age of one hundred still had clear recollections of soldiering in that waterless desert country. He was one English emigrant of the eighties who came over to be a cowboy, and, with the Army interruption, stayed with the life more than half a century. He never lost his zest for life, and was still painting landscapes of the country he loved near Grass Valley, California, very much surprised that he was more than one hundred years old.

Ken Ralston, of Billings, Montana, has become one of Montana's most noted western artists. He got his start before World War I, as a cowboy in eastern Montana during the last days of the open range. His personal researches and documentation of 1880's cowboys were very helpful in compiling data on the dress and equipment of the 1880's, and he has been a personal friend for twenty years. His paintings, sketches and models of historical Montana rank among the best ever created.

The letterhead from Montana's great western artist, J. K. Ralston

There have been more books about the open range cattle era than almost any other subject in the history of the West, perhaps barring George Custer. Many describe the history of the cattleman's glory days and empire of grass, few will tell you much about cowboy dress and gear of the 1880's. The following are some books recommended for further reading:

Abbott, E. C. and Helena Huntington Smith, *We Pointed Them North*. New York: Farrar & Rinehart, Inc., 1939.

"Teddy Blue" Abbott became a cowboy in the 1870's, and rode the northern ranges in the 1880's. His book of recollections has a great deal of what was real about the cowboys of his time.

Brown, Dee and Martin F. Schmitt, *Trail Driving Days.* New York: Charles Scribner's Sons, 1952.

A fine pictorial account of the open range era, with many excellent photographs of 1880's cowboys.

Foster-Harris, *The Look of the Old West.* New York: The Viking Press, 1955.

The most complete compendium on dress, tools, arms, and a host of other articles in use in the Old West, from the Civil War to about 1900.

Parsons, John E., *The Peacemaker and Its Rivals*. New York: William Morrow and Company, 1950.

The most complete book on the single action Colt and its chief competitors, Smith & Wesson and Remington.

Price, Con. *Memories of Old Montana*. Hollywood, California: The Highland Press, 1945.

Price became a cowboy in 1869. He worked the Dakota and Montana ranges in the 1880's, and stayed with the cattle business until retirement in 1922.

Rollinson, John K. (ed. by E. A. Brininstool), *Wyoming Cattle Trails*. Caldwell, Idaho: The Caxton Printers, Ltd., 1948.

Concerned mainly with Montana and Wyoming cowboys of the open range, much of the author's recollections apply to other areas as well.

Russell, Charles M., *Trails Plowed Under*. Garden City, New York: Doubleday & Company, 1927, 1948.

The famous cowboy artist's Rawhide Rawlins stories represent much of Russell's own experiences as a cowboy in the 1880's. One of the very best books about the open range cowmen of the eighties.